PLEASE OPEN THIS QUIETLY
HE'S PROBABLY ASLEEP

First printed and bound by
TDC, Southwark, London 2005

This edition published January 2006
By Exposure Publishing
An Imprint of Diggory Press,
Three Rivers, Minions, Liskeard, Cornwall, PL14 5LE
WWW.DIGGORYPRESS.COM

British Library Cataloguing In Publication Data
A Record of this Publication is available
from the British Library

ISBN 1846850193
978-1-84685-019-6

Also by the author:
Motor Tours & Walks, Scarborough

FOREWORD

Frank Taylor was born in 1911 in Scarborough, Yorkshire, to become the fourth and last generation of the Taylor clan to run a town centre business which has, in its time, dealt in stationery, printing, catering and fancy goods, since as long ago as 1848.

These are some of his superbly illustrated memories of the first 70 years, from bad times to good times, spanning a major world war and the development of modern technology.

A quiet and modest man, this book was written (and sketched) to record a stationer's life and observations through the twentieth century, and to entertain the following generations of his family.

It is an extraordinary story of an ordinary man, initially coerced into the family's struggling business at the age of fourteen, and having developed the business after his father's untimely death, being suddenly transferred into the alien world of war, India, and wireless telegraphy; then back again to family life and the 'shop', and finally into a busy retirement and further adventures.

Frank Taylor is now 94 years young and still lives in Scarborough, North Yorkshire, with his second wife Joan.

A big thank you to my son, Graeme, for many months of hard work, transcribing this book into a form suitable for publication and completing the process at his own expense.

Also, thanks to my wife Joan for proof-reading.

My life is now complete

Dormouse.

CHAPTER 1

So there I was, six years old, lying on my back on a very hard kitchen table with only a white sheet covering it. The doctor produced a wire frame covered in cotton wool, and sprinkled chloroform onto it over my face. He tried to convince me that it had a beautiful smell, but if that was what he enjoyed he was welcome to it, because it made my head ache, my ears sing, my heart race, and I saw all sorts of horrid fireworks before I eventually passed out. When consciousness returned I felt shocking, and was nursed all day by my mother, and by a hired nurse all night. It was considered normal in 1917 to be very sick after an operation and I certainly ran true to form in this respect, having just had my adenoids removed. "Its the best way to get rid of the chloroform" they said, but I can still smell the confounded stuff to this day, seventy years later.

Thank goodness my mother and father opted to have me "Done" at home, as I later discovered that the local hospital was a grim place with white tiles everywhere and smelling of anaesthetic and carbolic acid. There was no free medical treatment at that time, except for the destitute, and no doubt my operation was another debt which my parents would have to pay out of the very small profit which they made in the shop. The mention of that one word "Shop" has brought us down to earth with a bump. Class and social status have reared their ugly heads. Yes I lived over a small shop, and even behind a small shop, and my father was a Stationer.

Nowadays Stationer's shops simply don't exist in most small towns, but in 1917 the sale of pens, paper and ink was an

KITCHEN TABLE SURGERY

essential trade. Pencils and even slate pencils were there, but fountain pens and ball-pens were unknown. Your pen was in two pieces, the penholder and steel pen-nib which was the most scratchy and horrible thing imaginable. When later I had to master the art of writing with a pen at school, every desk had its inkwell and every boy had one or two penholders, and inky fingers.

IS HANOVER ROAD

The shop was in a narrow street near the town centre, with tram-cars passing the door and squealing round the corners in a way that can only be achieved by a tram with four steel wheels negotiating tight curves under protest. There was actually a War going on, now known as World War 1, 1914-1918, and I have a vivid memory of being pushed along

Hanover Road, outside the shop in a "Push Chair" with the shriek of shells passing overhead and the crash of explosions nearby. We were heading for the Waverley Hotel about 100 yards away, because they had a cellar and we had not. Later that day my mother and I left by train for Whitehaven in Cumbria because it was thought that the Germans might land at my home town of Scarborough following the shelling from ships off the coast, which was later known as "the Bombardment".

BOMBARDMENT OF SCARBOROUGH,
WORLD WAR I, RUNNING FOR THE
WAVERLEY HOTEL CELLARS

Other memories from that time include tin baths, peggy tubs, gas mantles, Dad's rifle and puttees (He was in the Territorials), and school.

TIN BATH AND JUG WERE STANDARD ISSUE TO HOUSES AROUND 1915

Gladstone Road Mixed Infants was my first school. It had a teacher who I thought was the most beautiful lady I had ever seen and a toilet which was quite the nastiest thing I had yet encountered. When my own children went there 25 years later that toilet was exactly the same, and even more nasty. A brick-built erection out in the yard, with minute windows but without toilet seats as we know them. Each small cubicle had two parallel planks of smooth wood with a big gap between them, and a constant stream of water running in a channel under that gap. The stream passed through each cubicle in turn until it mercifully disappeared at the smelly end of the loo. While my youngsters were there, this amazing contraption was replaced, using the more hygenic arrangement with which everyone is now familiar. But plastics had not really been invented yet and all loo seats were made of wood. Some were polished, some were varnished, and it was a good idea to make sure that the varnish was good and dry.

Why do I remember gas-mantles particularly? It was one day, or rather evening after the shop closed at 8 pm, when I was having a bath before the living-room fire. Above my head was a gas light burning brightly, when the glass globe shattered and everyone panicked to get bits of broken glass and gas-mantle out of the little boy's hair. That bath was called a "Sitz" bath and it was filled with hot water from a water-tank on one side of the black steel fireplace, plus the contents of a sooty black kettle which usually hung over the fire on a black hook. The other side of the fire was occupied by the oven, so I now realise that we had no gas-cooker, no hot-water taps, and of course no electricity at all. Gas lighting involved gas-mantles which were extremely fragile once they had been lit for the first time. They came in two sizes and gave light which was enough to read by, but only just enough.

IF YOU NEEDED GOOD HEALTHY EXERCISE, YOU COULD TURN THE HANDLE OF THIS FOR HALF AN HOUR.

The weekly clothes-wash was a great occasion. In the scullery was a built-in water-heater called a "Copper", consisting of a bowl of that metal set into a brick surround. The bowl was about 2' 6" in diameter with a fire grate beneath it and a large wooden lid on top to help control the steam.

BRICK-BUILT CORNER "COPPER"
IN AN "OUT-HOUSE"
AT 15 HANOVER ROAD

Other essentials were wooden instruments to get clothes out of the boiling water, and a "Lading can" to get the water out, plus a Peggy Tub with Peggy or Dolly.

ZINC BARREL WITH "DOLLY" AND
WOODEN TROUGH
STANDARD ISSUE TO HOUSEWIFE
PRE WASHING MACHINE ERA.

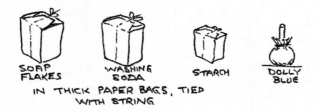

SOAP
FLAKES   WASHING
                SODA   STARCH   DOLLY
                                          BLUE
    IN THICK PAPER BAGS, TIED
         WITH STRING

To use this last item needed considerable strength, and we later acquired something called a "Posser" which was a much lighter, bang-up-to-date invention guaranteed to do a week's washing in no time flat. There was none of this nonsense about Truth in Advertising in those days, indeed there was much less advertising in any case, good or bad. Mostly it was in newspapers, backed up by bill-posting on hoardings and shop window displays. No radio, no TV, no electric or neon-tube lighting. all of which made for a quieter life.

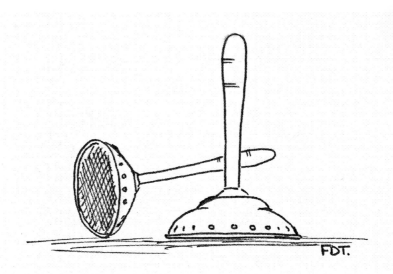

"POSSER"   THE LATEST HIGH-TECH AID FOR WASH-DAY'

But lots of horses made for a much more smelly life, especially on a hot summer day. Imagine a main street filled with horse-draw carts and carriages. Railway lorries with hefty shire horses, Brewer's lorries and Fish lorries also pulled by heavyweight animals. Horse-drawn cabs were everywhere and they had lighter weight animals, with the slenderest horse's legs seen on private carriages of great elegance. Scarborough's two department stores were Rowntrees in Westborough and Marshall & Snelgroves in Saint Nicholas Street. Both had doormen, resplendent in livery with top hats, and part of their function was to open carriage doors for customers entering or leaving their impressive emporiums.

But all these horses were normal healthy animals, performing nature's normal healthy functions all over the main street, and in hot summer weather the result was overpowering.

What to do about it? The answer was Street Cleaners and Water-carts. Not a perfect or complete answer, but it certainly helped. Corporation Cleansing Department men came onto the streets each morning with specially designed equipment consisting of barrows carrying two square dustbins, large brushes and shovels, and they proceeded to clean up the mess. The main shopping streets were provided at regular intervals with special wells on the pavement edge, each covered by a heavy metal lid about a metre square.

Horse-droppings were swept up and deposited in the wells under the pavement, and those wells were so hinged that they could be tipped out into the gutter when the "Muck cart" came round, and the contents were then shovelled into the cart.

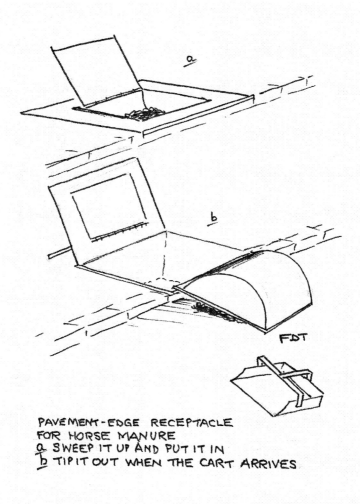

PAVEMENT-EDGE RECEPTACLE
FOR HORSE MANURE
a SWEEP IT UP AND PUT IT IN
b TIP IT OUT WHEN THE CART ARRIVES

The next excitement was the water cart, a square water tank on wheels (Pulled of course by a normal healthy horse) which washed some of the debris down the drain and left a little more from time to time, so that the work was self-perpetuating.

FDT

WATER-CART, WHICH FOLLOWED
THE "MUCK-CART", WHICH IN TURN
FOLLOWED THE CARTHORSES.

Soldiers in World War One wore Puttees, and I remember dad winding these awkward strips of khaki material from knee to ankle when putting on his Territorial Army uniform. Also he had a rifle and one clip of five dummy rounds of ammunition, and I tried to load and fire these five rounds, only to take a piece out of my left hand on the heavy bolt action.

Near to my school there was a little corner shop, kept by a bright little lady who was related to us by marriage, called Mrs. Tranmer. One day, while visiting the shop a certain inquisitive little lad wandered round behind the counter and disappeared through an open trap-door in the floor, where a flight of stone steps bounced him head-first into the cellar. The next thing I remember was being put into a horse-drawn cab and taken home. This was evidently a very serious occasion because usually we could not afford even tram fares, let alone hire a cab. The doctor was sent for again, and I remember him holding a candle in my eyes in a darkened room, but it seemed that all was well. My family thereafter blamed my shortcomings on being dropped on the head as a child. Quite understandable really.

HORSE-DRAWN CAB

FDT

Then the war ended and was soon followed by the Depression. Visits to my mother's home town of Whitehaven now found me in a new situation; men crowded the streets and squatted on pavement edges, sitting on heels all day. I was told they were colliers out of work because the pits had closed. Working normally in low coal seams down the mine, they found relaxation by sitting back on their heels, so this explained their surprising attitude on street corners. Women were there also, each with a black shawl over her head, and mostly in black clothes. This left on me a lasting impression of gloom and the feeling that something was badly wrong. I found it embarrassing that my Aunts were running a Soup-kitchen for the desperately hungry, but I did not even then realise how bad things were before the 'Dole' was introduced. Dole queues are a dreadful memory, but those pre-Dole days were even worse. "Good Old Days"? Not always.

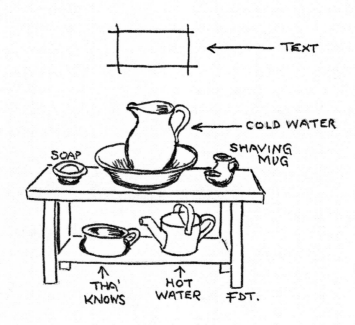

"WASH-HAND-STAND", BEFORE
"H AND C" IN BEDROOMS

When the War (W.W.I.) ended, my parents took a tremendous gamble, and bought a shop in a prime position in the main street of the town, involving them in a mortgage arranged by a solicitor, in the region of £3,500 at 5% per annum, plus a loan from my Mother's brother, Uncle Will, of less than £1,000. This meant great economies all round for some time, but we lived over the shop as before, and could look out onto the main street from our drawing-room (Now we called it our 'Lounge'). The vivid memory still remains of our first visit to those new premise. Everything from cellar to attic was covered by a half-inch thick layer of dust, and it took weeks, with the help of-two char-ladies to scrub every floor, landing and staircase. Gradually the living rooms were made habitable, and I realised that during the war years the place had remained unoccupied. Carpets came from an Uncle in the furniture trade. Few people then thought of wall-to-wall carpeting, so the square yards of floor-boards round the carpets were all painted with a preparation known as Brunswick Black, and then varnished. Landings and passages were covered by linoleum, and I began a new life in large high rooms in town-centre splendour. True, there was still the squeal of tram-cars objecting to turning corners, because all the town's tram routes now passed our door. The clang-clang of the tram warning bells punctuated the noise of wheels going over joints in the tram-track, and those 'Thuds' actually shook the whole building so that a more modern structure might well have cracked up under the constant battering. Most road traffic was still horse-drawn, although motor-cars were becoming more numerous. The idea of owning a car never occurred to us. People of our income and status did not have cars or telephones, which were the prerogative of Doctors and other professional men, and of course those who lived in large houses with many servants, and with chauffeurs. "People of independent means" they were called.

But there was such a lot to see from that window for an inquisitive boy as he grew from around seven years old. The road was paved with wooden blocks about the size of a brick, soaked in creosote and tar. The blocks had to he replaced every few years as the hooves of the heavy draught-horses bit into the wood, and the joints between the blocks were filled in with hot tar, the smell of which was with us for weeks while the slow process went on. Repairs to tram-lines were even more exciting, and were carried out late at night when the trams were all stacked in the Tram Shed off Scalby Road. A long pole was hooked over the overhead tram-wires and an electric welding arc was used for the repairs. In the meagre gas street-lighting, this was like continuous lightening playing down in the street and it lit up my bedroom so brightly that sleep was not easy. But I could sleep through most things even then, though the nickname of Dormouse did not appear until much later.

Beer barrels were delivered to the Pavilion Vaults by steam-driven lorries owned by the Scarborough and Whitby Breweries. This I could watch from the window and it was great! The lorries chugged up the main street, steam and smoke coming from the funnels, and red-hot cinders dropping frequently from the fire-boxes onto the wooden block roadway.

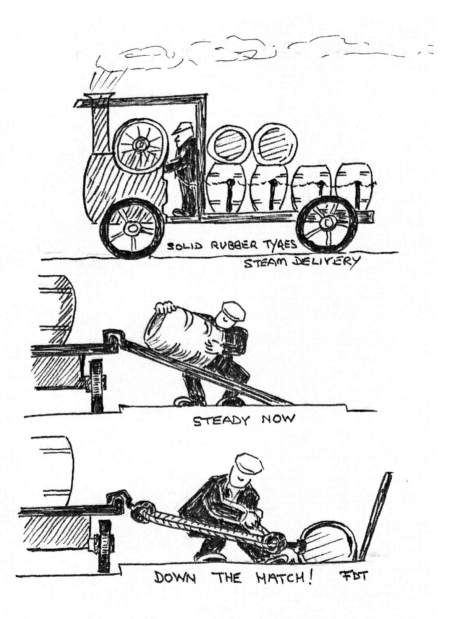

BEER DELIVERY

This caused occasional small fires of wood block and tar. No problem, there were always plenty of willing feet to stamp the fires out. Then a sloping barrel-slide was hooked onto the lorry side and one by one the huge beer barrels were slid sideways down the ramp onto the pavement; where a rope was rigged straight across the pavement through a ring on the lorry and used to lower them down into the cellar of the Pub. Empty barrels were hauled from cellar to pavement, and slung aboard the truck by two hefty Brewery men. It was all tough rugged work and there was usually a period of inactivity while the driver and his mate had a breather (And possibly a pint) behind the Pub's closed doors. Then off they chugged and I returned to my Meccano.

Meccano was a metal construction toy of immense value in the education of lads even up to 15 years old. One could discover more about the strength of materials, the best shapes for load-bearing, and the complications of gear-wheels and pulleys; than by any other means. Later my own son benefitted tremendously from Meccano in his turn, but sadly it is now made of plastic and much more clumsy for today's youngsters.

Among early motor cars were many Model T Fords. My school pall told me that they had three gears, Low High and Reverse, worked by a foot pedal and not by a gear lever. The steering wheel carried two levers with one controlling the throttle setting (No accelerator pedal I believe) and the other retarding the ignition to match the engine speed. All cars were started by hand, with a starting handle sticking out of the-radiator. Using this handle was a bit of an art. First one had to master the special grip, so that if the thing back-fired you escaped without a dislocated thumb. Then the throttle and ignition had to be set just right and choke if required. Looking very confident you then gave a great heave on the handle and nipped rapidly round to the driving seat to get control before the engine stopped again. But you did have the advantage of real motor horns which you were expected by law to give "audible warning of your approach". The horn with a rubber bulb and metal flared horn made a very satisfactory Honk, while the Klaxon needed a good strong bang on the protruding knob. which produced a squawk which would shift horses, hens or old ladies with amazing speed. Later there was a local car fitted with a pipe organ which played solemn chords, using the exhaust gases for power. The owner drove with cap reversed, wearing goggles, and played the organ with one hand while he drove with the other. That was status for him all right.

About this time I was moved to a small private school on the South Cliff run by a Mr. Helmsley. Not a success for me. as I was rather dim and very quiet. During play-time the standard form of amusement was to grab me and an equally insignificant youth called George, tie our hands together in front of us and tie the other end of the rope to the back of a cycle. George and I were then towed in a sort of unwilling race round the quiet square outside the school. I can't say that I learned anything at all at Mr. Helmsley's, except that the church clock nearby struck every miserable quarter hour until blessed release at 4 pm.

Back at home the large rooms had the latest form of gas lighting, with three smaller gas mantles in each fitting and several lights in each room to give plenty of light

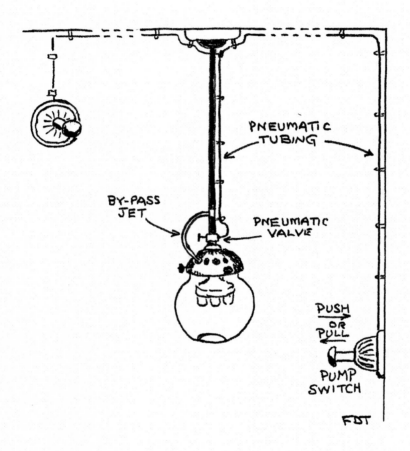

HI-TECH PNEUMATIC CONTROL FOR GAS LIGHTING, ON-OFF AT TWO SWITCHES c. 1920

There was a miracle of modern science involving one gas light in the shop, which even now I can scarcely believe. A pilot light burned continuously in the glass globe, and a pneumatic valve could turn on the gas to light the lamp and turn it off again. A very small-bore pneumatic tube ran from the valve to two small pumps, one located inside the front door of the shop and the other just inside the living accommodation on the first floor. So if we came home after dark, when the shop was closed, we pushed the front door pump once, and the light came on in the shop. Once upstairs in the house we pulled the other pump smartly, and the light went out down in the shop. You just couldn't get much more up to date than that! There was one tiny problem if the pilot light went out. It was then easy to turn on the gas supply and just leave it like that, and at that time gas came from the gas-works and was lethal, let alone the risk of explosion. But at that time more people injured themselves while lighting their gas cookers, while rarely if ever did we have those big gas explosions with multiple fatalities, due to gas leaks under the streets. Two possible factors could account for this, firstly the gas mains had not long been installed and would not fracture so often, and secondly when we smelt gas we were liable to go somewhere else as quickly as possible and report the leak knowing that coal gas could kill from carbon monoxide poisoning. Would it not be a good idea to make natural gas smell ten times worse than it does? Older folk lose much of their sense of smell and they would be less at risk, and even Dormice would be safer.

GAS LIGHTING OUTSIDE SHOP WINDOW
49 WESTBOROUGH,   c.1920

The whole shop was illuminated by gas, of course, as were all the streets in the town and even the Church which we attended as a family. Shop windows were also gas-lit, and in our case this was achieved by two very large outdoor lamps suspended about two feet in front of the shop window and well above head height. They also had pilot lights and one of my jobs was to go outside at dusk with the hooked pole, to pull down the lever which turned on the gas for each lamp.

In Church there were gas lights round the walls and also grouped in twenties or thirties in great chandeliers suspended from the roof. The caretaker has a very long pole, about twelve feet long in fact, with a wax taper at the end which he lit with a match. Then he turned on the gas to the chandeliers at one control tap under a seat in the central aisle, after which he applied the lighted taper to each globe in turn, and each lit up with a loud "Plop". One evening as a rather dull sermon dragged on, a small child discovered that one tap under his pew, and turned it off! The Minister could no longer see his sermon notes, so he dried up, and announced the last hymn. My father and I were doubled up with laughter (One NEVER laughed in Church) to find that the hymn was:

> The day Thou gavest, Lord, is ended
> The darkness falls at Thy behest...

Outside in the streets the gas lighting was controlled by clockwork mechanism inside each gas lamp. Scarborough Gas Co. workmen cycled round the streets every evening, each one with a ladder over his shoulder believe it or not, and checked the lights, because those in which the pilot lights had failed would pour gas out into the street all night unless they were either lit or turned off.

BEHOLD, THE GAS-MAN COMETH!
(MATCHES IN POCKET)

We were the proud possessors of a cellar in our new premises. Absolutely filthy it was, with one part reserved for coal, and a round hole in the pavement outside was fitted with a steel lid, so that the coalman could shoot sack after sack down into the depths and make a lot more thick black dust down there. The rest of the cellar had once been the kitchen for a Café, and a rope-operated lift had been put in to carry food up to the ground floor and first floor. Now we used it to take shop stock up towards the new stock-rooms in the attics. Great fun for growing lads.

CHAPTER 2

Things at school had improved a lot. Mothers and fathers realised that life was pretty grim for George and me, and we were both transferred to a Church of England secondary school called St. Martin's in Ramshill Road (Now Hunter & Smallpage, furniture shop). We were put into Miss Perry's class and we learned to call her "Ma Perry" when she was a long way off. A large lady was Miss Perry, with pince-nez glasses and a firm manner, but I am eternally grateful to her for noticing that this timid pupil might perhaps be a little less dim if he could actually see to read properly. So I was sent to the Opthalmic Opticians who found that I could only see the top letter on the chart with my left eye, and not a fat lot more with the other one. A pair of glasses was prescribed and duly arrived, gold-rimmed and with sides curled right round my ears. The school fees had to be paid, as had the sight-test and glasses bill, and I well remember wearing them for the first time. The whole street assumed an angle of about thirty degrees, down on the left and up on the right, and I had to take them off to get home safely. But help they certainly did, once I got used to them, and in a Year or two when St. Martin's School closed I was sufficiently normal in education to pass an entrance exam for Scarborough Boy's High School, where I spent the next few years.

The school summer holidays were, I believe, eight weeks long, and there was the attraction of permanent residence at a seaside resort. As a toddler, years earlier, I had been brought down to the sands and put into horrid scratchy

"Paddlers" which were splash-proof pants with a bib front. The scratched your legs and were no good if you sat

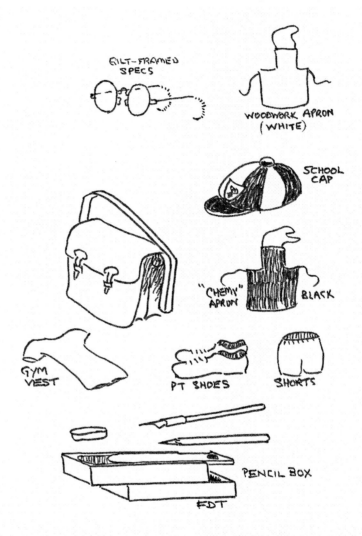

GILT-FRAMED SPECS

WOODWORK APRON (WHITE)

SCHOOL CAP

"CHEMY" APRON   BLACK

GYM VEST

PT SHOES

SHORTS

PENCIL BOX

FDT

SCHOOLBOY'S KIT c1925.   MUM AND DAD HAD TO BUY THESE, PLUS BOOTS AND CLOTHES, AND ALSO PAY THE HIGH-SCHOOL FEES.

down in sea, which I did! But now at eleven years old I could go down to the sands and wander about all day among the donkeys and bathing machines. I was never to use a bathing machine myself, but it was great fun watching people going in and out of them. They went up the steps while the machine was high and dry on the sands, and while they were undressing in modest retirement the Bathing Machine Man brought his shire horse which he hitched to the machine and towed it into the sea for a few yards.

BATHING MACHINE
FOR DECORUM ON THE SANDS

THE INTREPID SEA-BATHER

The bathers then emerged in costumes which covered everything except feet, ankles and head and came down the wooden steps into perhaps two feet of water. When they had ended their annual immersion they were towed back up the sands and could disembark, fully clothed, with elegance. How much all this cost I have no idea, but after all this was their once-a-year holiday.

As the years passed I went down to the beach with a few palls, and by then the Bathing Machines had gone, replaced by Bathing Tents formed up into a square and hired out to bathers by the local Council. Nowadays everybody just gets undressed on the sands, so the tents have disappeared also, but back in the nineteen twenties there were lots of things to see near the sea. We knew the Punch & Judy show word for word, and we knew the patter of the very red-faced ventriloquist who sat on the top of a pair of steps on the sands when he wasn't in the Lord Nelson. Catlins Pierrots were there on the sands as well and we knew their programme, and just when to move away before they came round with the hat. They had a special bag on the end of a pole and I do believe that Mrs. Catlin herself used it to collect money from crowds high up on the Spa Wall which overlooked the famous Catlins Pierrot Show. Shortly after this Catlins moved into a sea-front theatre, Catlins Arcade, the same theatre in which Norman Wisdom first donned his schoolboy cap which also became famous.

The Salvation Army did not escape our attention and we sang their hymns with gusto, but our loudest vocal efforts were in the open-fronted music shops of Francis & Day on the Foreshore. Two or three characters in striped blazers, straw hats and white shoes, sang the songs and played the piano at fff. When a crowd of youngsters had gathered, we did the singing while straw-hat brigade sold sheet music at prices ranging from 6d to 2/- each, or 2p to 10p in modern denatured currency, to the adult victims who joined in the big shout. Song titles I remember were "The Sheik of Araby", "Yes, we have no bananas" and "Valencia" but there were dozens more and we knew the lot. When we were hoarse we sought refreshment, which meant more hard work. Along the Foreshore were many penny-in-the slot arcades, and we made a systematic tour of every one from one end of the seafront to the other. We knew where to find those few machines which returned coins to successful players providing they pressed "Button B" as it were. So we pressed every Button B on the Foreshore and could usually find 2d each which was sufficient to buy the biggest ice cream sandwich in Scarborough, because we also knew the lady who sold them. She put a wafer into her special sandwich maker, and followed it with an inch layer of water-ice cream before putting on the second wafer and releasing the spring to eject the sandwich complete.

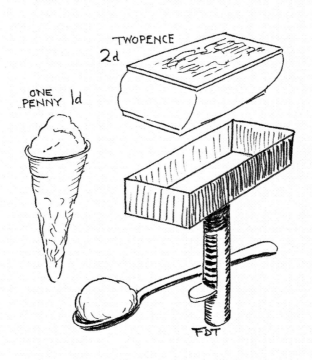

THE BIGGEST TWO-PENNY
SANDWICH, WITH THE HAND-
FILLING EJECTOR APPLIANCE

Then some days we would fish from the piers with a hand-line, if we could get some bait. We could go digging for sand worms, or collect mussels from the rocks at low tide, or perhaps part with our hard-earned Saturday Sixpence (2p). Thereafter we sat on the pier-edge with our legs dangling over the water, fishing line in hand. When we felt a bite we jerked the line to hook the fish, but most often this resulted in the bait being whisked away from the fish and only occasionally would we haul in a small 'Dab' or 'Par'. When tea-time was near, the line was wound back onto the square wooden frame, very carefully because the hooks were brutal, with sharp barbs which meant going to the hospital if you stuck one into your finger. Once I arrived home with eleven fish looped onto a piece of fishing line, which had nearly cut through my fingers with their weight. My poor mum had to try to cook them but they tasted rather like the bottom of the harbour, and soon after that I lost interest in fishing, having been given a new Raleigh Bicycle.

Yes, a brand new Raleigh, with three-speed gears and upturned 'North Road' handlebars and this was one of my life's greatest joys. Eventually it had a paraffin lamp on the front which was great fun, rather smelly, and gave very little light. Even later there were electric lamps which kept on going out and cost too much in batteries. I never reached the next stage which was a dynamo which rubbed against the side of the tyre, and gave a good light if you pedalled like crazy, but almost none if you were moving slowly. Wheel-hub dynamos came with new bikes, and I didn't soar to those heights of status-symbols. More your "Do-it-as-well-as-he-does-on-less-money" philosophy, which prevails in Yorkshire.

STRAIGHT OFF THE SANDS
ONTO THE BOAT FOR A SAIL

Just as today, inshore fishing boats worked out of Scarborough all year round, but during the summer months they would take visitors for pleasure trips. Most cobles (We in Scarborough call them "Cobbles") then had squarish 'Lug' sails on a single mast, and they came to the water's edge to ply for trade and embark visitors. Special gang-planks on two large wheels were pushed into the water beside the boat, and passengers walked up the plank to be helped aboard at the far end. Then the boat men pushed and 'Poled' the boat out, set the sail, and put out beyond the harbour walls. Once only did I go out for an hour's fishing. Never again. There was a goodish swell and I stood up in the bows having a smashing time on the way out. But when we anchored and started to fish, I lost interest in everything except seasickness, and just longed to be on dry land. Any land would do as long as it was stationary! The time passed slowly and I became much thinner before we came back ashore. Meanwhile my father and Uncle Ernest had enjoyed it no end.

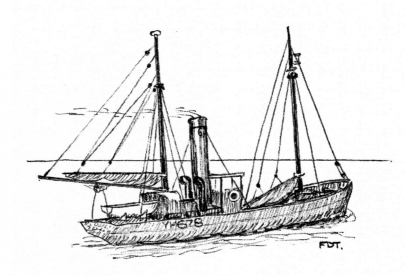

STEAM-POWERED FISHING BOAT

PADDLE STEAMER "BILSDALE"

Steam Trawlers fished out of Scarborough in those days, and they had a sail rigged aft. Drifters were rather smaller boats, driven by marine engines using oil, and then came the smallest of all, the inshore fishing cobbles.

The paddle-steamer 'Bilsdale' arrived each summer and ran trips up and down the coast for many years.

It set off two or three times each day carrying hundreds of passengers, with an accordion playing on deck and a well-stocked bar. You could tell whet the sea was like by looking at the colour of the passengers as they came back ashore. Pink for calm, white for moderate, and greenish yellow for rough seas!

A succession of other smaller passenger boats also worked out of Scarborough such as the White Lady, Yorkshire Lady and Coronia. While I was always reasonably happy on larger boats, small ones never attracted me much after that fishing trip. Dormice may sleep a lot but they do remember mistakes over very many years.

About the time when I was hurling down steep hills on my wooden scooter, there were Bath Chairs on the Esplanade in Scarborough. Bath Chairs were used by the aged and infirm around 1920. Like huge black Prams, with two large spoked wheels at the back and two smaller ones at the front. they were pulled along by an aged and bent Bath Chair Man, wearing a black suit and a bowler hat. The occupant of the chair was often invisible, as a black hinged pram-hood came well forward over head, and a black oilcloth cover protected the lower limbs from cold and moisture. It looked more like a horse-less funeral than a pleasure trip, but the Gentlefolk took the air in this way when unable to walk any distance, or just unwilling to do so.

BATH CHAIRS USUALLY SEEN ON
THE ESPLANADE, PULLED BY AGED
MEN IN BLACK SUITS.

Holidays away from home normally meant a visit to relations, as we could not afford hotels and did not much like boarding-houses. But when this involved a week or two in Whitehaven on the Cumberland coast, or in London at the home of my Uncle Ernest, two new worlds opened in front of me.

In Whitehaven it appeared that my relations, and even my mother, were on friendly terms with some very important people, and I was invited to go to the big house next door-but-one, and meet Mac. Gradon. Mac. was a few years older than I and very much taller. He lived in an enormous house with extensive gardens, a tennis court and a big summer-house which could be turned round to face the sun. We used to get it going round like a roundabout, and had to be stopped by the servants before we did untold damage.

An impressive driveway swept round past the main entrance, and there was a two-car garage which usually had standing outside it an immaculate Daimler car, driven and serviced by Gardiner the chauffeur, equally immaculate in grey livery, with shining black leather leggings and gauntlet-type gloves.

Mac. had the finest O-gauge model railway I ever saw, covering the floor of a huge garden basement room, and it turned out that he was mad-keen on railways. Sometimes he took me across the tennis courts and lawns of the garden and across the field beyond, to the railway line of the Furness Railway. We climbed the fence, crossed the line, and went into the signal box at Corkickle Station. I thought we were breaking the law, and I was scared, but the signal-man seemed to be a pal of Mac's and it was obvious that he knew the whole signalling and 'Staff' system for single-line working. Apparently Mac's grandfather owned a fair sized chunk of the shares of the Furness Railway, as well as the local newspaper, and Mac. was welcome anywhere on railway premises. Just imagine the thrill for a schoolboy to discover just how those signals and points interlocked, and the codes used by the telegraph which kept all the signal boxes in touch with the situation. As the train left Corkickle Station going North, it entered a tunnel which ran under the town and emerged at Bransty Station, Whitehaven's main station, and Mac. sometimes went onto the footplate and drove the train through the tunnel. Those were fairy-tale days, occasionally riding in the chauffeur-driven Daimler, and sometimes driven by Mac in the Rover tourer with the hood down. He would accelerate down-hill in the town, turn off the ignition for a few seconds, and turn it on again to produce and ear-shattering and window-rattling BANG which Mac reckoned (With some justification) would wake up a sleepy neighbourhood.

With a newspaper in the family it was natural that Mac. became a journalist, and he had the advantage of an excellent education. He later worked in a Manchester news-office, where I gather he met Alistair Cook of 'Letter From America' fame, but by then the fairy tale time was over and we lost sight of each other altogether. While at Whitehaven, we stayed with my Grandmother, Mrs. Fanny Dixon, who always looked exactly the same age. My early memories of Granny were of a dignified elderly lady with long black skirts sweeping the ground, a high-necked black blouse and a black velvet ribbon tight around the neck. When she ventured abroad she wore a bonnet, close fitting, which might sport a few purple tight-packed flowers. Her hair was always white and swept back into a neat bun at the back of her head. A powerful lady was Granny and greatly to be respected. She would preside at meal times but would never ask anyone to pass anything she needed. Her children (My mother, uncles and aunts) had been brought up to attend to the wants of others, and her grandchildren (Dormouse and his cousins) should behave in the same way -- or else! So Granny would stop eating, put down her knife and sit perfectly still. Slowly it dawned on us that something was wrong.

"Would you like some sugar Granny?"
"No thank you"
"Would you like some bread Granny?"
"No thank you"
"May I pass you the jam Granny?"
"No thank you"
(Pause for deep thought by everyone at the table)
"Shall I ring for Ella to bring some more hot water?"
(Things were now getting serious, whatever could it be ?,
"You don't seem to have a teaspoon Granny - have mine."
"No dear. ring for Ella, she has forgotten my teaspoon"

After which the electric atmosphere was dispersed and we all breathed again.

Granny usually wore a brooch which was in the shape of a bow of white ribbon and proclaimed her to be a member of the BWTA, the British Womens Total Abstinence, or Temperance Association. Granny had been brought up in the Anglican Church, but some time after her marriage she had been "Soundly converted" and transferred to the Congregationalists. Grandfather had meanwhile established an excellent business in making and selling furniture, much of which he designed himself. He had friends who were captains of small freighters plying between Whitehaven and the continent, and had built up with their help a stock of good cigars and a cellar of wines and spirits. When Granny was converted, she not only joined the BWTA, but she also poured every drop of Grandpa's wine cellar down the sink, and thereafter he had to go up the garden to the greenhouse if he even wanted to smoke a cigar or pipe. I can only remember seeing him once, but he was tall, stately and very charming, and I always considered he was a very big man to take all that and still stay with Granny. He must have loved her very dearly.

What do you think people did before the advent of the Hoover? Granny's maid used a Ewbank carpet-sweeper, which she called a "Boxbrush", and also an amazing hand-driven vacuum cleaner which needed two people to work it. One used to stand on the platform which projected from the base of the machine, and push to and fro a vertical pole which worked bellows to create suction. The other person guided the business end of the flexible hose over the carpet and chairs. The whole thing was most efficient, though rather labour-intensive. They had another suction cleaner, which looked like a fire extinguisher on a pole, but it was very little good at all.

The first time I ever heard a Wireless Set was during a visit to mother's brother, my uncle Ernest, who lived in Streatham and was among the top brass in the City of New York Bank in Old Broad Street. The receiver had no

HAND-POWERED VACUUM CLEANER, PRE-HOOVER, WITH DOUBLE-ACTING BELLOWS

batteries or mains connections, but consisted of a coil of wire on a 4" coil-former, with a variable condenser and a crystal which I think was of germanium, and which you prodded with a piece of wire called a "Cat's whisker". When you got everything exactly right, coil tapping, condenser setting, and cat's whisker, you could hear in the Ericson earphones the magic sound of London '2LO' Calling, coming to you from the B.B.C. at 3 Savoy Hill behind the Strand. And it was just that; sheer magic.

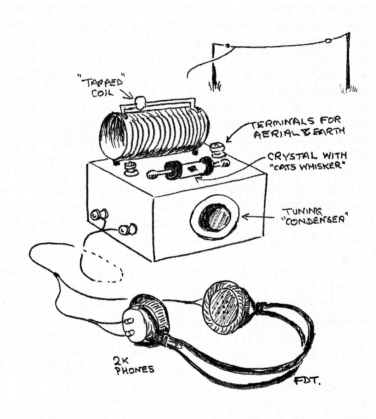

"TAPPED" COIL

TERMINALS FOR AERIAL & EARTH

CRYSTAL WITH "CATS WHISKER"

TUNING "CONDENSER"

2K PHONES

FDT.

CRYSTAL-SET.
NEEDED NO BATTERIES BUT
LOTS OF PATIENCE!

Later on came Wireless sets with Bright-emitter valves which could amplify signals to loudspeaker volume, and if you owned the luxurious Three Valver, would give enough light to read a newspaper by. Two forms of power were needed, known as High Tension (HT) and Low Tension (LT) batteries. The HT were 120 volt Dry Batteries, with tapping points at low voltages to provide grid bias to the valves, but the LT came in the form of an accumulator which needed charging every two weeks, necessitating two visits to the local wireless shop or garage. It is difficult to believe, but true, that when I joined the RAF in World War Two, there were still sets in use which needed accumulators and batteries, and we had not yet heard about such things as transistors, so everything worked on radio valves, though by now they were Dull Emitters which gave no useful light at all !

Granny had a valve set of course, after the war. The most modern type which was mains operated. At Christmas the whole family gathered in her spacious lounge, which had four enormous windows, to hear the King's Speech. The servants were called in as the time drew near, and stood at the back of the room, Big Ben chimed the hour, the band played the National Anthem, and we all stood to attention until the very last sound of the Anthem had faded. Then we sat motionless to hear our King speak to the Nation and Empire, and woe betide anyone who moved.

3 VALVE WIRELESS, WITH H.T.,
L.T. AND 'CONE' SPEAKER
BRIGHT EMITTER VALVES
AND SWINGING COILS
1 STAGE HF, DETECTOR,
AND ONE STAGE LF, NOT
VERY STABLE

There was another Great Wireless Occasion, which was one of the biggest flops of all time. Beryl's father was going to speak on the Wireless from London. As before the family was summoned to the lounge. While we are all sitting there waiting for zero hour, I should explain that Granny's youngest son, my Uncle Laurie, had married a mysterious lady called Beryl. My Uncle Laurie was no other than J.L.Dixon, author of at least one book on Antique Ceramics, and London Manager of BTH (British Thompson Houston Co), a very sophisticated gentleman of faultless manners and urbane presence. His wife, Beryl, was scarcely known to the family, though she had been north to Whitehaven once or twice for a visit. It was thought that she was of French nationality, though when I met her during the war she seemed to have no trace of an accent.

So now the wireless set was switched on and the announcer (Probably wearing a dinner jacket) introduced Beryl's father to the waiting millions. The voice which now emanated from that speaker had a rough uncouth Yorkshire accent, even worse than mine, and lacked all grace and refinement. No one spoke. The air was electric. Everyone was perfectly still; then Granny reached down to the skirting board beside her chair and pulled out the power plug which supplied the wireless set. Regaining her faultless composure, she said that it would be a good idea to go to Ennerdale straight away. as it was such a nice day. Beryl's father was never mentioned again as far as I remember, and we went to Ennerdale Lake to expunge him from our memories.

It was in Whitehaven, when I was only around six years old (or even less probably), that my Mother took me to visit a very important lady called Miss MacGowan, and we were shown into a very dark room, with huge dark plush curtains and portier curtain, aspidistras and tall plant stands, and for the first time in my life I heard mechanically reproduced music. There in the half light dark wooden cabinet, perhaps a yard high by about half that wide. Set into the front of the cabinet were two doors which opened to reveal more darkness, and the domed lid was hinged to lift upwards. The clockwork mechanism required winding by means of a handle which fitted into a socket in the side of the case, and the 'Voice-box' on the 'Tone arm' was lowered onto the rotating gramophone record. It hissed and it coughed, and out came the strains of a recorded orchestra. I was NEVER AGAIN INVITED to visit Miss MacGowan, because at that moment I disgraced myself by howling at the top of my voice at that dreadful noise. Of course it was the first time I had heard recorded music, but if that was what an orchestra sounded like they could jolly well keep the Albert Hall for all I cared!

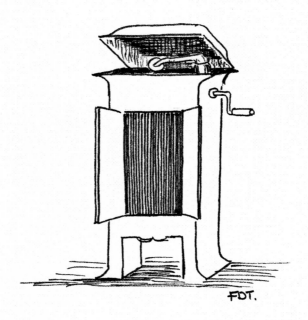

THAT HORRID MACHINE

CHAPTER 3

Back at home again after a holiday at Whitehaven, let's have a conducted tour of 49 Westborough which was our shop and home, as it was in the early twenties.

The ground floor was all shop. Stationery was our basic trade and our stocks included pens, paper and ink, plus account books and all sorts of Stationers' Sundries. The rear of the shop was a very small wholesale warehouse supplying the nearby villages and towns. The first floor consisted of lounge, dining room and kitchens. The lounge you have looked into previously, it was very high, with a big bay window overlooking the main street. The cornice between wall and ceiling had a plaster-cast decoration of flowers and leaves right round the room. A central pendant gas-fitting hung from the middle of a similar circular decoration at least a yard across, and two more gas-fittings stuck out from the chimney breast.

There was no electricity, that came later. A restrained art-deco tiled fireplace was put in before we arrived, although we continued for some time to use the traditional cooking-range fireplace in the dining room behind the lounge. Later, this was pulled out and its successor was a dark oak surround and mantleshelf housing a tiled hearth; a dark oak kerb completed the picture. My mother was then doing pewter-work as a hobby and she made a pewter panel to fit the vertical area beneath the mantlepiece, bearing the words "East West, Hame's Best". (Which at present hangs in my daughter's house).

LIVING-ROOM FIREPLACE AT 15 HANOVER RD AND FOR SOME YEARS AT 49 WESTBOROUGH PRE-DATED ELECTRIC KETTLES, HOT-WATER SYSTEMS, GAS-COOKERS AND CENTRAL HEATING

From the dining room, one door led directly onto a flat roof which covered the rear of the shop premises. The flat roof was surrounded by a square of four-storey hotel and shop buildings so that sky could only be seen if you went close up to a window and looked upwards. A large chimney constantly poured out smoke into this square, from the Pavilion Hotel kitchens and heating system. Only a short distance away, the steam engines in the LNER railway station added clouds of smoke as they built up a head of steam to commence their journeys, and the prevailing wind brought that smoke straight to us. No wonder the place was dirty when we bought it!   .

Two smaller rooms were used as kitchen and scullery, and the latter had a flat stone sink in it when first we arrived, with one tap only, for cold water. Should you want hot water it was quite simple to heat it in a kettle on the fire or on the gas cooker. No electricity meant no electric kettle or immersion heater. The flat stone sink was later replaced by a deep white ceramic sink and then we had the luxury of hot water from a small gas water-heater mounted on the wall over the sink.

Up another flight of stairs, were three bedrooms and the bathroom. But you must not miss the bathroom! The hand-basin boasted a gas water heater like the one in the scullery, but the piece-de-resistance was undoubtedly the so-called "'Geyser" which provided hot, or nearly hot, water to the bath. Standing on a hefty wooden stool, it was the size of a narrow hot water cistern, made of copper and with a six-inch flue pipe from the top of the Geyser to an external pipe. If you dared to light the thing, the process was complicated. First there was a pilot gas jet to be lit, which projected a six-inch narrow flame outside the heater housing. Because of interlocking levers, the water supply had to be turned on next, before the final dramatic climax. Now the burning pilot jet could be swung round to throw its flame into the inside of the machine, and this action automatically turned on the main gas supply to the twenty jets which heated the water.

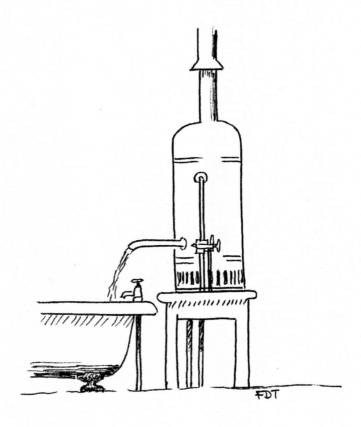

"GEYSER" WE INHERITED ON MOVING
TO WESTBOROUGH IN 1918.
IT LOOKED HARMLESS ENOUGH,
UNTIL YOU LIT IT!

For a few seconds nothing happened, then there was an
almighty HURRUMPH ! The big heavy bathroom windows
rattled, and everyone in the building knew what was going
on. After this it was a matter of adjusting the flow of water to
get water to run as hot as possible. The warm water

emerged from a horizontal pipe about half way up the heater, and which stuck out so far that the only safe place was the opposite end of the bath, to avoid gashing oneself on the sharp pipe end.

Life was much less exciting (But considerably safer) when the Geyser was removed in favour of a multi-point Ascot water-heater. Now for the first time there were two taps on each hand basin, bath and sink, and when any 'Hot' tap was turned on, the Ascot burst into feverish activity, heating the water as it passed through machine with a lot of hissing and groaning.

A year or so later we had, a new toilet fitted, which had a low level cistern. The old toilet had the cistern way up near the ceiling, with the then conventional lavatory chain and ceramic dangler at a convenient height. But unfortunately the new toilet was connected by the plumber to the wrong side of the Ascot Water Heater, and we then had the only toilet in Scarborough which flushed with hot water! Copper water pipes were now being fitted, but all the original plumbing was in lead pipes, and as a youngster I used to watch my friend Mr. Tate the plumber, light his blow-lamp and 'wipe' a bulging joint on lead piping with great skill, using a mole-skin for the job. Incidentally, Mr. Tate was the first man I ever knew who could make his own valve-driven wireless sets, his loudspeakers were hand made cones of special fabric which he 'Doped' with shellac, which I learned to do later on because the only alternative was a horn speaker which was too expensive on my pocket. Like most families, we had a wooden pole in the back yard, with about

100 feet of copper aerial wire leading via egg-shaped insulators to a lead-in tube passing through the window frame. Another wire went to a copper earth rod driven into the soil, and just inside the window was a double-pole double-throw switch to connect the aerial to the earth during a thunder storm, and which must always be left that way when we went on holiday.

When first we moved to the main street in 1918 there were no milk bottles. The milkman called every day with his horse and cart, and on the back of the cart was a large shining milk churn with a tap on it made of shining brass. He filled a portable can from the churn and brought it to the door where one of us would meet him with a jug which he filled using measuring cylinders which normally hung down inside the can. He was paid cash there and then. Much later the milk bottle appeared and later still one could buy 'T T Milk' (Tuberculin Tested) which was a great luxury mostly used for feeding babies.

Looking back, it was a wonder that so many of us survived the hazards of everyday life. Lead piping must surely have caused lead poisoning, horse-manure was spread liberally over the streets every day, milk could easily be contaminated, our only protection was vaccination, and no one paid any attention to radiation risks when X rays were used for demonstration in school, diagnosis of fractures, or for shoe fitting in every shoe shop in the town. Added to which, some of us jumped head-first down cellar steps, so you should consider yourself lucky (Or very unlucky) that the Flying Dormouse lived to tell the tale. (or tail).

BEFORE THE AGE OF
BOTTLED MILK AND SLICED
BREAD.

went to school in Harrogate, one of his friends contracted the disease. Certainly that boy was isolated for some time in hospital and certainly all the school had diagnostic treatment, but before long the invalid was back at school and perfectly normal. We may grumble at the present day health service sometimes, but the oldies among us know how lucky we are. Perhaps not so much lucky as indebted to all the medical scientists have sweated away their lives to advance the frontiers of science and to save our lives even after they were dead.

To change the. subject, have you ever heard of an 'Out-porter' ? No? Then hear ye, hear ye. When all the trains in Scarborough Station were steam-hauled, there was a staff of railway porters in uniform on the platforms. Passengers arriving by train would ask a porter to take their luggage from the luggage rack or from the guard's van, and carry it to the station forecourt. This they normally did using a two-wheeled barrow of a special heavy design, or a four wheeled truck which would take a dozen suit-cases if things were busy, and a tip of three or six pence (1-2p) was expected for this service. Once outside the station, the railway porter could only summon a cab or an 'Out Porter'.

On the road outside that station yard there was a rank where usually about half a dozen barrows stood with their owners in attendance and each owner had fastened round his arm a large cast metal badge bearing his own number and 'Out Porter' ' which was issued by the local Council. It was just as well he had that badge, as otherwise you would hesitate to hand over the luggage of your worst enemy to most of them.

INSIDE THE STATION

OUTSIDE THE STATION

PORTERS MET EVERY TRAIN, AND
"OUT-PORTERS" PLIED FOR HIRE ON
A RANK OUTSIDE THE STATION

But visitors who could not afford a cab would put the family luggage aboard one of these barrows and follow it carefully, never letting it get out of sight until it arrived at their holiday hotel or apartment. Here the Out porter would receive his fee of a few pence plus a few pence tip if he was lucky, and he would look around to see if anyone with luggage was going back to the station. Saturday was a busy day for him, but on any other day he might be hired by a commercial traveller, to transport a couple of big wicker hampers full of samples, which completely filled his barrow.

Now there's another thing I bet you wouldn't know about. Having a main-street shop, we were visited by the 'Reps' or Representative of all the main suppliers to the stationery trade, such as John Dickinson, Newton Mill, Mabier Todd (makers of the Swan Pen) and dozens more. These were men who had to uphold the dignity and prestige of their firms, and I remember more than one who arrived in top hat and morning coat with all the presence of a Viceroy. A few years later it was bowler hat and pinstripe suit, and later still each rep brought his samples in the firm's car, and wore a neat lounge suit with rolled-brim hat or wide-brimmed trilby. But those original grandees in top hat and frock coats had their samples brought into the shop by the Out Porter, and they would move from shop to shop as a sort of double act with the rep. returning at night to the Pavilion Hotel next door to us, one of the most prestigious hotels in town. The Pavilion Hotel was run by the Laughton family, whose most famous son was Charles Laughton the actor, who was therefore my next door neighbour before he rose to fame, and years before I achieved the doubtful distinction of being a flying dormouse.

In the 1920's I had never heard of supermarkets, and food was always bought through smallish specialised shops such as Grocers, Butchers, Bakers and Greengrocers. Every Wednesday a certain Mr. Wray called on my mother for "The Order". He was our Grocer, and he would also deliver the groceries on Thursday on his bicycle. He would appear every Wednesday morning, wearing a bowler hat, white apron, and in cycle clips, open his stiff-backed note book, and turning his eyes up to the ceiling would reel of a list of his stock items as an aide-memoir, always ending up with "Pepper, salt-mustard-vinegar-black-lead and boot-polish". His cycle had a large carrier above the front wheel which held a proper grocery basket, just about big enough to hold a week's groceries for an average family. Soon after this we had a delivery cycle of our own and I was the one who normally rode it. Big heavy awkward thing it was, too, and it was very easy to get the front wheel in the tram-lines and finish up on the roadway.

Before refrigerators made their appearance, we had to cook meat and fish the day they were bought, and things like milk and butter would "Go off" in hot weather if left too long. Rooms known as "Larders" were fitted with stone slab shelves and were kept as cool as possible to store food. Other rooms outside in the back yard were the coal-house and the wash-house, and there might be yet another for coke. We had a new house built around 1950, and the plans had to include outside coal and coke stores, to supply fireplaces in lounge and dining room, plus partial central heating. When I had a heart-attack these were all converted to gas to avoid my wife Marjorie having to carry coal and coke in addition to running the business herself and doing all the housework, while I sat around doing nothing in particular and doing it very well.

Back in my school days, my pals and I could be found on Saturday mornings in summertime on a wide-topped wall in Westwood, overlooking the railway lines running into Scarborough Station, watching the constant stream of excursion trains which brought "Trippers" to the town, and which were hauled by engines from distant railway systems, such as Great Northern, Midlands, Lancashire-and-Yorkshire, Great Western and so on. Our own line was the L.N.E.R. and our favourite engine locally was a 4-6-2 tank engine which pulled the train between Scarborough and Whitby, a beautiful and very hilly line, now a country path for walkers, which only had customers in the high season, so never made much of a profit. But the great thrill on Saturdays was to see the big Pacific 4-6-2 engines and the Atlantic 4-4-2 come gliding into the station, and we never dreamed that steam would ever be superseded by any other form of traction. To us, the drivers of these magnificent machines were real men, and far more important than politicians or film stars. Few of us knew the names of footballers, even though they were featured on cigarette cards.

Outside in the streets, steam-powered delivery lorries were not the only vehicles with solid rubber tyres in those far off halcyon days, because I travelled on a local bus which had solid tyres.

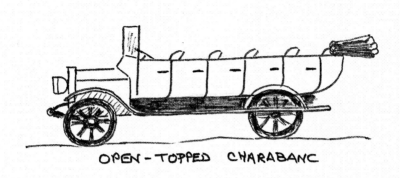

OPEN - TOPPED   CHARABANC

OPEN - SIDED "TOAST-RACK"

Now and then, we had a holiday in Scalby, about 4 miles out of Scarborough. That is to say, my parents had the holiday, while I had to travel to school each morning on the Peoples Bus Service and join the 'Country boys' for lunch in the school kitchen, on payment of 'Dinner money' of course. Only boys who came into Scarborough from the countryside were provided with meals, as local lads could all walk home at lunch time and there was always someone at home to get a meal ready. Most families consisted of Dad, Mum, youngsters, Aunts and Grandparents, and it was very strange if there was no one who could get a meal ready. Should there be a widow with a child, there would always be a relative or neighbour who would give the little one a mid-day meal if mum was at work. Being compelled to pull together as a family or as a neighbourhood was not such a bad thing. Social Security and Pensions may make us all more independent, but it also tends to fragment basic social groups.

Mind you, that Scalby Bus was a beauty! It looked like something out of a Keystone Cops film. Dark brown in colour, it was low at the front and high at the back and you went up a series of shallow steps as you made for the rear seat.

SCALBY BUS c1925, WITH SOLID
RUBBER TYRES, NO HEATING, RATTLING
WINDOWS, AND TOP SPEED 25 M.P.H.

A bonnet at the front covered the chugging engine, with the starting handle sticking out permanently below the radiator, as was the case with most cars at the time. Self starters had not been invented, and on each side of the bonnet were the usual mudguards, each with a large brass oil lamp on it. Behind the bonnet, a vertical glass windscreen was made in two pieces, with a horizontal join across the middle, allowing the top half to be opened outward and upward to enjoy the fresh air in summer. The driver could open the passenger door by means of a large lever each time he found a customer. And find them he did! There were no bus-stops of course, so every hundred yards or so he would give what the police described as "Audible warning of his approach". This was achieved by pulling yet another lever, which clapped a thing like a train-whistle over the end of the exhaust pipe. The sound which this made was unmistakable, a sort of throbbing whistle unlike any other noise in the countryside. There being no 'transistor set' in any house, in fact no canned music of any kind, folk near and far could hear the bus and put on their hats and coats and walk down to the main road in the comfortable knowledge that the bus would be doing a good fifteen miles an hour and would be along soon. When they got onto the bus they paid the driver, but no tickets were needed because he owned the bus and tickets were a waste of money. Conversation was not easy on account of the noise. Every alternate window was made to open like the windows in old railway carriage doors, so the glass pane, in its hefty wooden frame was a loose (very loose) fit in a vertical channel. A Thick leather strap with holes in it was secured to the bottom edge of the window, and if you heaved on that strap, the window came up out of the lower part of the door and you slipped the holes in the strap over a brass stud on the outer frame to adjust the height. So every alternate window was very loose and rattled unmercifully at each bump in the road. The tyres were rock solid, the springs were rock solid, the road was designed for horse-and-cart use and was a matter of mud and grit held together by pot holes. When this vehicle worked up to a stupendous 20 mph, therefore, conversation was not difficult, it was impossible. The calf and chickens dumped on the back seat of the bus didn't like it either. Someone usually put farm produce or livestock in through the back door somewhere along the route which added to the entertainment value of the ride. We did all keep dry if it rained, but if the weather was cold it simply meant that the passengers were cold too, as car heaters were non-existent. The three mile trip cost three old pence (1p) but a schoolboy travelled at half price. As I write, the same journey costs around seven shillings and sixpence (37p), an increase of some 3,700 %.

If you were a little girl, and if you ate the last piece of bread and butter on the plate, you were told that you would get "A handsome husband and a thousand pounds a year". You would then have lived in luxury all your life, and the very thought of the Old Age Pension of £1862 which I now enjoy could not possibly have been believed at that time. Mind you, this was also a sneaky way of getting little girls to eat bread and butter.

When that old Scalby Bus eventually reached Scarborough it would back slowly into the Balmoral Hotel Yard in the town centre and await passengers for the next trip. Yards were used by other busses and carriers carts. The latter were horse-drawn carts which plied at least once a week between outlying villages and the town centre for the transport of goods, parcels and farm products. It usually fell to me to get heavy parcels from our shop to the carriers cart at (Say) the Sun Inn Yard, and I did this on the firm's cycle, as did most so-called 'Errand Lads' at that time, giving the driver three or six pence to take the parcel to Cloughton or some other address. The horse which pulled the cart knew the route so well that the driver would often fall asleep once clear of the town, and rumour had it that one driver, having taken aboard even more beer than usual at the Sun Inn, rolled off the cart into the hedge-bottom while the horse went quietly on its way home. Someone noticed that the driver was missing, and in due course a search party was sent back down his normal route and found him snoring in the ditch. If it rained, there was a tarpaulin which was tied down over the load, and some carts had a metal cage erected over them about six feet high, which supported a canvas covering.

The delivery of goods to shops from manufacturers was quite a different process at the time. Very few suppliers had their own delivery vans coming into our town, and most shop stock arrived by Goods Rail, with more urgent or lighter parcels by Passenger Train or something called "Sutton's Transport".

Every day a mixed goods train would come into the Goods Yard in Falsgrave Road, where parcels were off loaded, listed, and put onto flat delivery carts which were then pulled by beautiful shire horses which were stabled in Sherwood Street. Each morning the driver would harness up his horse and lead it up Falsgrave to the Goods Yard. If they felt a bit skittish (The horses I mean) they would rear up on their front legs and kick out with their hind legs just for fun, and one day I was cycling past one which did just that and the massive hoof was only inches from my face so that I felt the draught on my cheek. If that horse had been just a bit more skittish you would not have had to read all these reminiscences.

So the Goods Rail Cart would arrive at the door of our shop with a couple of oversize barrels or crates of pottery. How to get whacking great crates down from the cart to the pavement without breaking the contents? Answer, a sloping ramp made of heavy timber, hooked onto the cart at one end and resting on the pavement at the other. All hands would help the driver to ease the barrel or crate down the slide and onto his sack-barrow to move it into the shop. If it was too big to go through the door, it had to be unpacked on the pavement and the straw put back into the container in time for the lorry to take the "Returned empty" on its way back to the yard. There was a special cheap rate for this Returned Empty category and packings were re-used many times over.

Then for super-speedy delivery we would receive parcels within two days, or even on the day of despatch, by Passenger Rail.

GOODS RAIL DELIVERY LORRY

CARRIER'S CART, DRIVER ASLEEP!

These parcels travelled in the guard's van of normal
Passenger Trains, and were delivered from the Station by
the inevitable horse and cart which made its daily delivery of

parcels which were usually smaller than Goods Rail items because the charges were greater for this very quick service. They were only allowed to carry parcels, and not correspondence which must go by post. So when I wished to send photographic negatives by Passenger Rail, I had to pack them up to look like a proper parcel with string round it in two directions and a label on it to prove that it really was a parcel. Sellotape had not been invented, and would have proved nothing anyway, but I could see my negatives right onto the train, phone the addressee at once, and they would collect the 'Parcel' at Leeds station and have the negatives in their factory within two hours all told. Bet you can't beat that even today.

In between Goods Rail and Passenger Rail came a mysterious system known as "Sutton's". Some firms sent all their deliveries by Suttons, and this is how it worked. Suttons lorries collected the supplier's parcels and charged them a bulk rate, then put them into a covered rail wagon which was attached to the back of a passenger train. At main-line stations Sutton's men would sort and trans-ship parcels to other wagons to provide a nation-wide service. In each town served by this system, was a "Sutton's Agent" with horse and cart bearing the official inscription on the tail-board, and all this was quicker than Goods Rail which took one or two weeks, but not as quick as the Passenger Rail performance. Whichever system was used, the lorry driver had a list of parcels on his lorry, with addressees and sender's names, and we had to count the parcels (Often 20 or 30 from one supplier) and sign the way-bill as a form of receipt. Goods damaged in transit involved the recipient claiming from the carriers within a very few days, and keeping both goods and packings for their inspection. There was a special cheap rate called "Owner's Risk", so if you were sending six heavy hammers which would not damage if dropped, you would use this rate and save expense.

CHAPTER 4

Scarborough High School for Boys was in the Valley Gardens, close to the Valley Bridge. At the time I was there, the bridge was being rebuilt and the steam driven pile-drivers pounded away for months to find a firm footing for the stone piers. Then the noise of the pneumatic riveters seemed to last most of my school life. We could always see red-hot rivets being passed from the forge among the girders, to the riveting crews.

One morning there was a powerful thunderstorm and the school was struck by lightning, with me in it. The classroom was full at the time, when there was a tremendous blue flash and a simultaneous BANG which I believe knocked me out. The next thing I remember was coming too to find an empty classroom, and setting off to try to locate my missing class mates. It's not everyone who has fallen down stone cellar steps and been struck by lightning before leaving school.

How easily the faces of school teachers come to mind after 60 years have passed. The geography teacher was known as "Rubber-jaws" because he had difficulty in pronouncing the letter R. The French master was called "Pish" because he spluttered a great deal, and those in the front row got a shower bath. Maths was taught by a very short teacher who was smaller than most fifth-formers and was naturally "Titch", while English was drilled into us by "Snaff". To a

man, they all lacked a sense of humour, and it was a
wonder that we learned as much as we did.

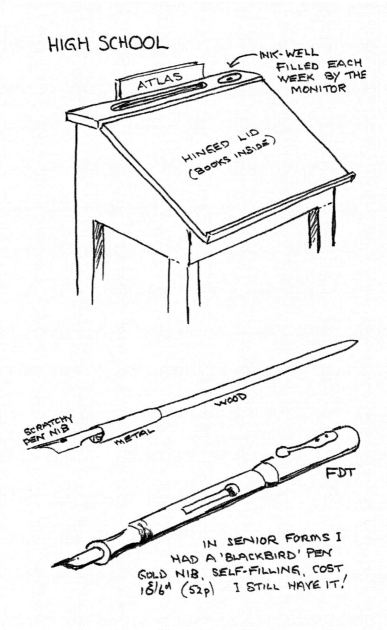

HIGH SCHOOL

INK-WELL FILLED EACH WEEK BY THE MONITOR

ATLAS

HINGED LID (BOOKS INSIDE)

SCRATCHY PEN NIB

METAL

WOOD

FDT

IN SENIOR FORMS I
HAD A 'BLACKBIRD' PEN
GOLD NIB, SELF-FILLING, COST
18/6ᵈ (52p) I STILL HAVE IT!

It was only in my last year at school that I realised that I could actually acquire knowledge by actively learning things myself, rather than by having them banged into my unreceptive skull by perspiring schoolteachers. The Chemistry master was "Buggy" Walsh, a man for whom I had the greatest respect. He had a Blue Book which recorded detentions. Known as "Walshes Tea party" this entailed staying in the Chemistry Lab from 4 to 5pm and working under his eagle eye. Not far away on the top floor was the Physics Lab, presided over by the benevolent but jumpy "HH" who could explode with fury at any instant. Down in the basement was Squires who taught woodwork "Square-the-end-to-measure-from" was his constant plea. Also "Brad" Bradley who always wore white flannels and taught gymnastics, but dormice are not a lot of good in a gym, and completely useless at football and cricket.

Buggy Walsh later had an accident in the chemistry laboratory when an explosion resulted in one boy being blinded for life. The boy was John Wilson, son of a Methodist Minister. That boy became Sir John Wilson, President of the Commonwealth Society for the Blind, and through his work thousands of blind people have had their sight restored. But the accident deeply hurt Mr. Walsh who suffered under the memory of it for the rest of his life.

As I remember it, the Valley Bridge before my school days was very narrow. Two carts could just pass each other comfortably. Horse-drawn cabs moved at a gentle trot, and the steady clip-clop of the hooves caused the whole bridge to move up and down so that if you stood in the centre of a span you were going up and down rather too far for comfort. If my memory is correct, a Government grant was made for the new bridge, on condition that an access road of equal width was built later both to the north and the south. Indeed the road northwards was built, now called Northway, but World War 2 came along in 1939 and the project was lost to sight. Cynics would say that building an access road to the south would have devastated the South Cliff area where many influential people lived!

At the school in which I was struck by lightning, I twice obtained the five credits necessary to pass my Matriculation Exam., but in both cases I failed to pass in English Composition, so ended up with two School Certificates. Spelling and punctuation again took their toll. That same building became the Stephen Joseph Theatre in the Round, used as a workshop and springboard by Alan Aykbourn, and has never since that day been struck by lightning. Subsequently, both my son and daughter had difficulty with spelling, and my belief is that this is the thin end of the wedge, the thick end of which is dyslexia. So I have always had a fellow feeling for people who find it difficult to read. Nothing gave me greater pleasure in life than the day when my son, Graeme, received his doctorate at a ceremony in the Albert Hall. dressed in all the magnificence of the Lord Mayor in a proper floppy hat. My daughter also achieved teaching Qualifications at college, and both of them had trouble with spelling, bless them.

Today's school-children are taught to think in metres and centimetres, which may be ideal if they are going into science or will live in Germany or France. It is a dead loss if they are to live in England and want to buy curtains or jam, which obstinately stay in yards, pounds, pints and so on. Incidentally feet were used long before metres were invented, with the organ pipes in the days of J.S.Bach (1685-1750) which were measured in feet. with organ stops known as 8 foot, 16 foot etc.. The A4 paper on which I am pounding this script is shown on the packet as being 11¾" x 8¼", and who asks for 454 grammes of jam?

Another huge confidence trick was the conversion of British currency from £.s.d to metric, when I noticed that a lettuce which cost 6d before the changeover, cost 6p after it, an immediate inflation of 240%. Much time and money could have been saved by dual pricing and dual weight marking, with this country sticking to its existing currency. It failed to bring us any nearer to parity in coinage with any continental country. A bit like the Humber Bridge, leading from nowhere to nowhere else, but wanted by politicians as a means of gaining votes. Rum lot politicians.

My mother's father had seen his wine poured down the sink, but not so my father's father, who was himself quite a character. As a small boy I was commanded to "Kiss Grandpa goodbye" when we visited him, and I can still remember two things very clearly he had a grizzly beard which I liked not at all, and a distinctive smell which I encountered nowhere else. That smell I later learned was whisky, and it seemed that Grandpa was hooked on the stuff and was also a man of great determination so that he was rarely without an adequate and generous supply, no matter what else was lacking. He had come to Scarborough years before from Bedale in Wensleydale, and had set up a shop which just would not be possible today. It was in Eastborough, where now there is Jaconelli's Cafe, and had narrow double doors of Victorian design.

PRE WWI GRANDPA TAYLOR'S SHOP STATIONERY ON THE LEFT, BAKERY TO THE RIGHT

Inside, one turned to the right for home-baked bread and cakes, and to the left for stationery and printing. The three sons of the family were each taught a trade; my Uncle Reginald was a printer, Uncle Edgar was a baker and confectioner and my father was a stationer, which was then a viable trade and livelihood.

So I guess Grandpa reckoned he had it all fixed in order to take an early retirement and let the lads do the work. His business was thriving, the firm published a local ABC Railway Guide and also Taylor's Almanac full of local history, information and anecdotes. His bakery specialised in Simnel Cakes which were despatched all over the country (So the advertisements said) and they carried out catering for special occasions and at Officer's Messes at their summer camps.

But there was, so to speak, a snag in the ointment. It was my Grandpa's liking for a tot of whisky, or two tots, or three. To cut a long story short, he drank the whole business to ruins. His sons could see the inevitable outcome of this, and all left to find employment elsewhere, and the original firm had to close down. My father took a job in Whitehaven, as a commercial traveller for Mosses in Lowther Street who were stationers and dealers in wrapping and printing papers. Nearby was Dixon's Furniture shop, and dad met my mother, Jane Dixon. They were married and came back to Scarborough to start a tiny retail and wholesale stationery business which was my home environment as a very young child.

But Grandpa Taylor continued to do pretty well at emptying whisky bottles, and ended up in what was known as a "Dwelling" which was provided as a charity in recognition of his former services to the town, which I understand included the formation of the North Side Golf Club. For many years my father provided a sum of money each week which kept the wolf from Grandpa's doormat, but none of the rest of the family agreed to help, and this drain prevented dad's business from growing as it should. It was found that, instead of paying for groceries with this money, Grandpa was investing it in "The hard stuff" so arrangements were made whereby we paid Chapmans the Grocers for a weekly supply to be delivered to his door. This worked well until we learned that he was flogging the groceries and drinking the proceeds.

No wonder, then that my father was a total abstainer, as was my mother, and very early in life I decided to avoid spirits because it seemed possible that I might have inherited a tendency to get hooked on it like dear old Grandpa, and it wasn't worth experimenting to find out. I never did like the taste of beer, or even the smell of it, so my drinking is limited to the occasional half of cider, or a sherry, mostly at celebrations.

But back in High School days, I was rather unconcerned about all that, and more involved in cycling around the countryside and failing to achieve great heights academically. Brought up on Meccano and enjoying physics and chemistry at school, it was natural that I became interested in making my own valve-driven wireless sets (Not known as "Radios" then, and long before the transistor was invented) and I got a very basic knowledge of the theory of wireless which came in handy when I joined the RAF during the war, and became the Flying Dormouse.

One of my school friends adapted a pendulum clock to work from an electric battery. He fitted an extension to the pendulum, about half way down, which formed the moving core for a fixed solenoid. A very precise lever and notch arrangement switched on a pulse of current to the coil which gave an impetus to the pendulum to maintain its motion. This only happened when its action declined to a fixed minimum , and to me the whole thing was fascinating. It went for years and for all I know may still be going. Leslie Guppy who made it became a telephone engineer and did pretty well in that extremely technical work.

After the cycling years came the walking holidays. These started at Methodist Holiday Homes. which cost me about £7 a week, and had daily walks of five or so miles, then on to CRA Centres which thought in terms of ten or fifteen miles including two or three thousand feet fells, and then to independent walks with a friend. Standard walking gear was known as "Plus fours" and was a not-too-baggy form of knee breeches with hairy long stockings. Fell boots were unknown, and we wore a pair of "working boots" of brown leather and had climbing nails put right round the welt and in the instep and round the heels, with more nails all over the soles and heels. They then weighed a ton, but could get a grip on rocks and boulders which was very useful. A long yellow oilskin cape covered not only the walker, but also his Bergen rucksack inside which was food. clothing, primus stove and billycan. To top it off there was a Balaclava hat plus a black Sou-Wester (which until recently still hung in my garage). The rain poured off the oilskin onto the trousers and stockings, and carrying around 50 pounds weight there was so much honest sweat that nothing was the least bit dry.

Once I spent two weeks in Scotland with Charles Burrows. Charles was a club cyclist and an all-year-round sea bather. Fortunately he was also very patient, because I was a non-starter as an athlete. One day we started from Ratagan Youth Hostel, Shiel Bridge, and did the ridge walk of the five Sisters of Kintail, all up around 3,000 feet, and we intended to stay the night at a farm in the glen running down to Glenquoich.

HIKING OUTFIT, PRE-WW2

Each farm we got to was completely deserted, and we tottered into the village of Glen Quoich only to be told that the local Laird (an Englishman) would not allow anyone to put us up for even one night, not even on the floor of a barn. We humped our rucksacks onto our backs again and staggered off down the road in a sort of daze of disbelief and some five miles further on we were picked up by a travelling grocer, who no doubt could see us literally wobbling about the road.

That grocer's car held two Scots who looked exactly like Laurel and Hardy. To me they were heaven-sent, and I remember seeing some whacking big deer wandering along the road and then I rather think that I must have passed out or gone to sleep in true dormouse fashion. Next day I just dragged myself along, but after that I began to enjoy it all again. We must have covered about 36 miles, including six peaks and carrying packs which weighed a good 50 lbs.

CHAPTER 5

There were trams in Scarborough from 1904 to 1931, so I grew up in the Tramcar era. Most short journeys were one penny or two pence (The old penny with 240 to the pound) and you could go all round the town on a circular route for sixpence. Of course these were real TRAMCARS, with open top-decks and open platforms at each end for driver and conductor. Right through the winter, those drivers stood on their platforms and faced hail, rain and snow, clanging their foot-operated warning gongs to clear the way. At places where line junctions necessitated "Points", there were pointsmen who carried heavy steel levers five or six feet long, which they jammed into the points and heaved sideways, so that the points moved from left to right with a typical "Clonk", a sound then familiar to everybody but now only heard in tramway preservation lines. There were some points in isolated places which were unmanned and then the driver slowed down to walking pace while the conductor jumped off the rear platform with his own point lever, ran and overtook the tram, operated the points and swung back aboard as it gathered speed again. As a boy, I was fascinated by the tram brakes which seemed to be a two-way system. Huge steel brake shoes could be applied to the rims of all four wheels, and central between the front and back wheels there was a large brake shoe which could be lowered with enormous force straight down onto the steel tram track. This could almost lift the tram clear of the ground, and everybody slid forward along the shiny wooden seats which ran down each side of the lower deck. In spite of all this, a tram did run away down Vernon Place (Later renamed Road) and ended up in an underground entertainment complex called "The Aquarium"

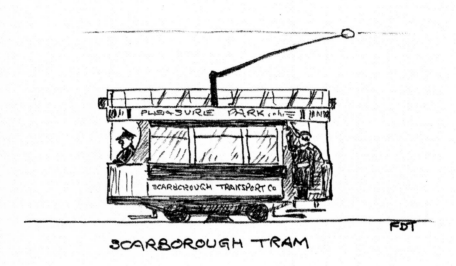

SCARBOROUGH TRAM

When a fully loaded car ran down North Marine Road it lurched and swayed downhill towards the Floral Hall, where the lines simply ended without anything to check the hurtling monster. I often got off at the cricket ground and walked the last bit rather than risk continuing down the open road towards Peasholm Lake. If the lines were iced up or extremely greasy, there was a box full of sand and a pipe leading down to the leading edge of each road-wheel, to help it to better grip on the slippery surface.

From Scarborough trams, my mind takes me to those in Nottingham, where I was sent to the shop of a certain Mr. Court to learn the trade of Stationer. Trams passed the shop door, and one winter day I put on my coat when the shop closed, and jumped on a tram as it started to climb the hill, quite slowly, on my way home. I sat down on the long wooden seat which ran the length of the car on each side. People on the opposite side noticed smoke coming out around me. and I could smell fire and brimstone and guessed that the brakes were overheating, assuming that the smoke was coming up from below. It wasn't till a couple of days later, when I reached into my pocket for a match, that I knew what had really happened. The matches were all burnt out inside the charred matchbox, so if ever you should jump onto a tram "when the car is in motion" and swing inboard against the vertical pole on the platform, don't do it hard enough to ignite that box of matches in your pocket as I did. Come to think of it you couldn't do it today if you tried, because the modern tram has doors which only open when the car has stopped. All the fun of leaping on and off tramcars has gone for ever.

In Nottingham I had learned how to repair known makes of fountain pen, and how to die-stamp hand made notepaper, and I subsequently took examinations organised by the British Stationer's Association. I also learned what a lonely place a big city can be, even though I did go to a Congregational Church and met lots of local people. Guess I must have been a pretty obnoxious animal, especially when I developed a skin complaint which was traced to my visits to a Swimming Bath. However, it was soon cured by the doctor, and I eventually returned to my home, wise in the crafts of the Stationery Trade.

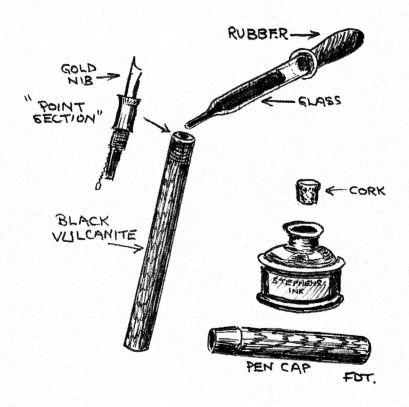

GOLD NIB →

" POINT SECTION"

RUBBER →

← GLASS

← CORK

BLACK VULCANITE →

STEPHENS INK

PEN CAP   FDT.

EARLY 'SWAN' FOUNTAIN-PEN FILLED BY USING A PEN-FILLER (2d) AND BOTTLE OF INK

At about this time I visited quite a number of Scarborough Churches, from Roman Catholic to Quakers, because I was dissatisfied with religion as seen at the Bar Congregational Church at which I had been brought up. This tour ended in my becoming a member of the Methodist Church, where

Christianity was a challenging religion meant more than whist drives and badminton. After a year or two, and with far too little training and education, I was allowed to preach and take services in local churches and also those further afield when the Young Laymen's League organised events in neighbouring Circuits.

Before leaving school I had a secret ambition to be a laboratory chemist, but I was not clever enough to get one of the few exam prizes which carried monetary grants, so there was no chance of me going to college or university because my parents could not possibly pay the fees. Then I also knew that my father and mother had both of them worked their whole lives to build up a good business, and there was only one Dormouse to carry on, so carry on I did. My starting wage was five shillings and sixpence a week (22½p), most of which I gave to my mother towards housekeeping.

That would be around my fifteenth birthday, and some five or six years later I had to run the business along with my mother, as father died after a prostatectomy when only 56 years old. If antibiotics had been invented, he would probably have survived, but sadly at that time there was no medication available to control peritonitis.

As a child I had learned to write on a slate. It was held in a flat wooden frame, and dangling from it on a string was a piece of damp cloth. With it was a slate-pencil, made of a stony material about 6" long by about 1/8" wide, bound around with paper for half its length. This made a mark on the slate, and also made a squeak which set teeth on edge. The wet cloth acted as an eraser, and the object of the exercise was to avoid the use of paper which cost money, so children could play and learn without expense. Perhaps schools today have gone just a bit too far in the opposite direction.

INFANTS SCHOOL

SLATE PENCIL

Slate

WET RAG

I LEARNED TO WRITE ON A SLATE (BUT NOT TO SPELL)

Later I sold slates and slate-pencils, so they were still used seriously. or as toys at least, around 1926 when I started work. The next step for children was to use pencil and paper, and finally pen-and-ink which was very advanced stuff, and an exercise book at school was an important possession, not to be soiled or blotched with ink. All exams now carried the stock instruction "Neatness and spelling will be taken into consideration". Ominous for Dormice. whose little paws were always dirty, and who could never spell anyway.

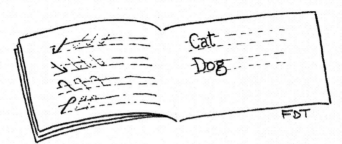

COPY-BOOK   SHAPES ("POT-HOOKS") AND LETTERS HAD TO BE COPIED FROM THE PRINTED EXAMPLES, USING A SCRATCHY STEEL PEN.

In a Stationer's shop the penholder was usually displayed on a card of twelve, secured to the card by loops of elastic, the penholders, like paint-brushes, pencils and fountain-pen fillers, were known in the trade as "Carded goods". These were also available at village shops and small corner shops, as were bottles of Stephens Ink (Blue-black) and packets of Stationery (A few sheets of paper and some envelopes at 2d), plain postcards, pads, envelopes and "Compendiums" (Pad plus envelopes in a cardboard folder).

Mention of pen-fillers reminds me of the first so-called "fountain pens". The ink had to be put into the hollow body of the pen using a glass dropper/with a rubber bulb. Then the nib section had to be replaced and screwed home tight, and the pen was shaken hard to persuade the ink to flow onto the nib. The nibs were of gold with minute iridium tips which either wore down in time or broke off, involving the purchase of a new nib, usually fitted by the stationer. I learned how to fit nibs, and repair bent ones, and to do many other repairs to pens at the repair department of Mabie Todd & Co Ltd, near Oxford Circus.

To be a Stationer in my days one needed to take examinations in the mysteries of the trade. Paper for writing and printing was made in a series of sizes with ancient names. Foolscap, Post, Large Post, Crown, Demy (To rhyme with "The pie'), Albert, Imperial and Double Elephant come to mind, and each original size folded in half became "Folio" e.g. "Cap Folio" for Foolscap Folio. Folded twice it became Cap Quarto and folded again it was Cap Octavo and there were also 12mo and 16mo sizes even, and the size of each had to be known in inches. Even now most folk know that a quire of paper is 24 sheets, but reams are, or were more tricky, with a ream of 480 sheets in writing papers, but reams of 500 sheets in printing papers to allow for 20 mistakes in printing. Most printers used hand-fed machines, and it was easy to make a mistake. It was dangerous too, as my uncle Reg. found when he lost the end of a finger on a machine which naturally had no protection for the operator's hands. You had to be quick and accurate in those days. By the way, twelve dozen is a gross and seven gross is 1008. Bet you didn't know that either.

Self-filling fountain pens arrived soon, with Swan and Waterman being the early contenders, both filled by a lever set into the barrel of the pen which compressed a rubber "Sac" while the nib was held under the surface of the ink in the bottle. The sac would perish in time but could be replaced by the Stationer. Who had special tools and a tube of rubber solution which he usually bought at the cycle shop. Conway Stewart pens catered for the cheaper end of the market in gold-nibbed pens, and one day a new traveller showed me the cheapest fountain pen ever. The Mentmore Manufacturing Co had produced a self-filling pen with a steel nib turned up at the end, and packed in a beautiful cardboard box individually, to sell at one shilling and three pence (About 6p). Later on I sold them in grosses, the famous Platignum Pen.

One of my friends at that time was selling dress materials by the yard at "One eleven three", which was his shorthand for "One and eleven pence three farthings" or I/II¾. (i.e.l0p per yard), and he had cheaper stuff at half that price. Burtons would make you a suit to your personal measurements for £3 and there was another firm known as 'Fifty Shilling Tailors' who would do it even cheaper. Of course £2.50 was more than a week's wages to some folk. I certainly remember street urchins without shoes in mid-winter, and that was not because they liked running about in the cold and wet without anything on their feet, but because there was no money to buy even canvas shoes. A shoe shop in Victoria Road had a contract to supply the Workhouse in Dean Road with dozens of pairs of boots. If you were flat broke, you could go to the Workhouse in any town, and get something to eat and somewhere dry to sleep providing you did so much work to help keep the place operating. But you must not stay more than three nights, so there was always a few Gentlemen of the road moving on to the next town and begging a bit of food or an ounce of tea on the way.

GROCERS SHOP WITH YEAST AND TWIST

At the grocers shop or chemists there was soap. Real soap was made from animal fats and caustic soda, and could be tough on dirt and rather too tough on the hands. Knight's Castile was white and Carbolic was red, both came in big chunks about 31/2" x 21/2" x 2" in size. Char ladies would scrub floors using a scrubbing brush, a block of this soap, a bucket of water and a kneeling mat for a little over a shilling an hour (6p), and as rubber gloves were not thought of their hands were rough and red, poor dears.

Also available at the Grocers were such basic requirements as :-

1. Washing soda in thick blue paper bags.
2. Blue-bags. Little cloth bags about 1½" across, full of "Dolly blue" which was used in the final rinse of your "whites" in the Dolly Tub. Advertised on hoardings "Out of the blue comes the whitest wash" (Reckitt's Blue).
3. Soap flakes in paper bags, to melt easily in the tub.
4. Robin Starch, to stiffen shirt collars and cuffs.
5. Monkey Brand, a block of abrasive powder which would scratch the hide off a Rhino.
6. Pumice Stone, even more abrasive.
7. Black lead, to polish up your steel fire-grates.
8. Donkey stone, to put a white edge on the back door step.
9. Fire-lighters and fire-wood, to light the fires.
10. Vim scouring powder, then without added detergent.

The grocer bought many items in hundredweights, weighed them out into llb or 2lb paper bags, tied down with string because Sellotape had not been invented. So it was with sugar, butter, flour, currants and so on, and always on the counter was a block of brewer's yeast, sold by the ounce, and in the country there was paraffin, treacle and milk for those who brought their own jugs to be filled by the grocer.

Persil detergent is supposed to have appeared first about 1906. but it did not reach us until much later than that, and green Fairy Soap was later still (But well before we heard about Fairy Liquid). All grocers had a display of biscuits in big square tins with sloping glass lids. so that one could see the contents. Everything, but everything, passed through the hands of the grocer's assistant, and by the end of the day those hands could be very grubby. No rules at that time ensured washed hands when handling bacon, ham or sausages. It was only later that pre-packaging arrived for such items, and they were then often labelled as "Untouched by the human hand".

Across the road at the chemist's, there were more treasures. Pear's Soap was oval, transparent, and kind to the skin, and had a very early advertisement carrying a picture of an over dressed little girl "Preparing to be a beautiful lady" with another asking "'Did you use Pears Soap today?". For the teeth there was Gibb's Dentifrice, a flat tin containing a block of pink stuff on which you rubbed the toothbrush, and which "Defended your Ivory Castles" (So they said). We preferred Kolynos toothpaste, which tasted of minty soap and filled the mouth with froth. But my teeth were a never ending source of income to a series of dentists both before and after the National Health Act.

Have you ever "Put down" eggs? Eggs were always scarce in winter, even non-existent when there was a war on, so we bought a lot when they were cheap in the summer, and "Put them down". This involved buying a tin of Waterglass (Sodium silicate) at that chemist's shop, mixing it with water, and pouring it into a bucket or pot full of eggs. They didn't go bad, but were not as good as farm-fresh eggs except for cooking, and at least you had eggs when other people had none.

Wax Vestas, they were matches made with short lengths of wax taper in place of wood. More expensive than the wooden sort, they burned longer, but tended to spoil the taste of a pipe-full of tobacco unless you smoked pretty strong 'baccy' like Black Twist. Black Twist was for outdoor men like fishermen and farmers. Twist was coiled up on the counter of the tobacconist, or at the corner shop, with a knife hinged to the counter in order to chop off an ounce, or half an ounce which went straight into the tobacco pouch, unless SHE was buying it for HIM among the weekly groceries. Men preferred not to do shopping, that was Women's Work. Incidentally, one of the things that tapers never did in my lifetime, was to taper. All those I ever saw were the same width from top to bottom, but perhaps when they were dipped by hand years earlier they must have narrowed off at one end. Useless information is just about limitless, isn't it.

Coming back to our own shop, there were account books which were required by every business and profession before the advent of mechanised accounting and computers. Ledgers, Cash Books, Day Books and Journals were the main items, mostly in Cap Folio size, about 13" x 8", and half-bound in Red Basil (Leather), ruled usually in Single or Double Cash or English Ledger which carried Debit and Credit both on one page. In addition you could buy Analysis Books with up to 52 columns across the opening, and special rulings were made to order. Larger and smaller books were stocked in a variety of rulings and bindings, from full-bound Red Morocco (Goatskin) to paper-backs!

Then Loose Leaf Account Books made their appearance. Now if you wanted to falsify the accounts, then a Loose Leaf System was specifically designed for the purpose. An all-night sitting fiddling the figures could be disguised beautifully by replacing a few pages in the books, at least this was the opinion of the Old School who would not buy them. But the Young School sure did buy them, together with new Loose Leaf Billing and Wages Systems, and there were good continuation orders for specially made refill sheets in quite expensive packs.

You might think that legal documents and correspondence had been typewritten ever since Hadrian signed the contract for a wall from Carlisle to Newcastle. Not so. Ever heard of "Copying Ink"? Henry C.Stephens & Co Ltd used to make it, and we supplied it in half-pint stone bottles to solicitors. We also sold the special Copying Books with water wells and brushes, so you may "Well" ask "How did it work ?" All will now be revealed to an enthralled (Bored) audience.

First you needed a lawyer's clerk, about 70 years old, a quill or steel pen, and a piece of vellum or hand-made paper. The clerk dipped his pen into Copying Ink and in faultless copper-plate script wrote the letter or document. He then took down a Copying Book, a thick leather-bound ledger-like tome with pages of copying tissue. One sheet only was moistened with water and then laid down on top of the document to be copied, and oiled boards were put in place to separate this pair from the rest of the book.

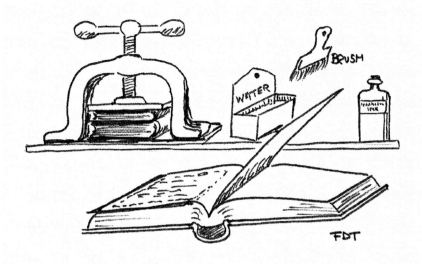

COPYING - BOOK WITH WATER-TROUGH,
BRUSH AND BOOK-PRESS.

The book was closed and put into a Copying Press and left all night under great pressure. Next morning there was a perfect copy in the copying book which became a permanent record of the legal transaction. Yes all this did really happen during my lifetime. Photocopiers are more convenient, though more expensive in investment and not so good at relieving unemployment.

Copying ink pencils could be used in the same way but were less effective, and were normally used as an indelible pencil, and every schoolchild was taught Never to lick the pencil lead as dreadful things would happen if they did. Another thing which the child must NEVER lick was a paintbrush, because these were often imported from the far east where lethal infections like anthrax could contaminate them. At school, all really good brushes were labelled 'Camel hair', and it was only later when I became an agent for Winsor & Newtons artist's suppliers that I found that they just did not make brushes from the hair of camels as it is far too coarse and wiry. These days there is more emphasis on Truth in Advertising.

One more useless piece of information I remember, My father used to suck a throat sweet which was a very small pellet of chlorate of potash. Sometimes he would keep a few of these loose in his waistcoat pocket, and also at times he would carry a few loose safety matches in the same pocket. Those matches could 'Strike' on the cough sweets, so I was taught to separate potash sweets from matches. Bet you didn't know that!

Talking about matches reminds me about Indian Matches. It was important to strike Indian matches away from oneself and certainly not towards ones face. The wood of which they were made was never straight-grained. Result, they broke in half five times out of ten, and the brightly burning business end of the match flew off anywhere it liked, usually onto clothing or down the neck of a shirt if it could.

I haven't seen a peashooter for yonks. Time was when every lad had a pea-shooter. and I was no exception, though my mother hated it as she was brought up before such dirty things existed. I would go to a Corn and Seed Merchant and buy a "Pennorth of Carlings" which were very hard small peas. Put a dozen in your mouth and blow them through the peashooter and you could hit a window, or a bowler hat. or the glass of a gas-lamp or anything else within range. Great fun for a penny. But then I only had three pence a week pocket money, and there were aniseed balls. liquorice sticks, humbugs and shoe-laces to be considered. Shoe-laces were strips of ridged liquorice about a foot long which could be torn into lots of long black strips like shoe laces. There were also chewing gum and penny sherberts, but these were sinful and wicked, were frowned upon by my dad and mum, so usually avoided by me.

Had a scooter about that time, I did. Made of wood with solid wooden wheels and solid rubber tyres, it would do quite a surprising speed down the paths in the Valley Gardens, and I used to put the heel of my right boot (Not shoes in those days) against the rubber tyre of the back wheel to act as a brake to avert instant catastrophe. My boot developed deep grooves in the heel as a result.

CHAPTER 6

Around 1936, my mother and I bought our first motor car, a Super Standard Nine, at £168 complete and on the road. There were cheaper cars than VN 7239, as one could buy a new car for £100 at that time, but that Standard was our pride and joy. We used it for business and pleasure, and it got very used to the journey to Whitehaven. You could have any colour, as long as it was black, and it had brown leather upholstery, four-wheel brakes (Many cars had brakes only on rear wheels) four doors, running hoards, self-starter, and a windscreen which was hinged at the top and could be opened by pushing the lower edge forward at the turn of a handle. This allowed fresh air to reach the passengers in hot weather, but there was as yet no way of heating the car in cold weather. You just put on more clothes – simple! Trafficators were built into the uprights between the front and back doors. They were orange-coloured arms which hinged out of the car horizontally and lit up when you twisted a switch on the dashboard, but did not self-cancel (That came later). There was a starting handle which could be pushed into a hole in the front, to start the thing in cold weather or if the battery was low, which often happened in winter. Every 5,000 miles it had to be decarbonised (De-coked) by removing the cylinder-head and chipping carbon from the upper part of the cylinder area. Using upper-cylinder lubricant, which was put into the petrol, it was possible to reduce wear on the cylinder walls, but eventually you needed a re-bore to return them to circular shape, and incidentally increase the power a bit. What that would cost nowadays would involve a second mortgage, so we now buy a new car instead. Mass production for planned obsolescence is a stupid philosophy.

"STANDARD 9" COST £168 NEW, AROUND 1938, WITH RUNNING-BOARDS, SYNCHRO-MESH GEARS, AND FOUR-WHEEL BRAKES.

I had learned to drive a car already, taught by a friend from schooldays, Denis Middleton, who is still a pal of mine after all these years. He owned a Jowett car, an open tourer which would climb a chimney. Yes it did actually climb a hill then known as Rosedale Chimney, which was One-in-four and full of hairpin bends to boot. Not only that, but it did it uncomplainingly on two cylinders only, because the engine had two horizontally opposed cylinders and a huge flywheel which gave a wonderfully smooth action. But the gears were not smooth. and had no synchro-mesh, so you needed to double de-clutch and rev the engine to agree exactly with the road speed of the back wheels before engaging a new gear. If you could change gear on that Jowett silently, then you could cope with anything a gearbox could throw at you. There was a hand brake which worked by tightening a band round the outside of the brake drum and had little if any effect, and a footbrake which did the same on the transmission shaft and would snap it in half if applied too hard. I remember we once sailed through a bunch of stray cattle near Ruston, unable to stop, with Denis driving and me fending off cows by leaning out and shoving them away as we drifted past. Going down steep hills was a high-risk art, and we had that car up and down one-in-three hills frequently.

The very first time I drove for any distance, we found ourselves going up Limber Hill at Glaisedale, with me driving. It's a one-in-three-plus-hairpins job, is Limber Hill, and both Denis and I were having kittens, but the trusty old Jowett went chug-chug-chug all the way up. If we had to stop, the brakes could not possibly have helped us from running off backwards, and I dread to think what would have happened. Rather fewer dormice I guess.

We paid cash for the Standard Nine of course. It took a lot of doing as we probably lived on about £350 a year, but Hire Purchase was a rude word, and the only arrangement of that kind we would consider would be a Building Society scheme on property. For any other purchase it was normal to save up for it and then buy it. Certainly if your credit was good you could go to a shop or a craftsman and get credit, but it was the accepted thing to pay in one month. If word got around that you did not pay promptly, then the shopkeeper regretted that "They had no account in your name". It must be admitted that some very influential customers would abuse this system, delay payment as a matter of course, and were actually being financed by tradesmen to whom they owed so much for so long.

Computers had not been thought of, and banking was effectively much quicker! If for instance I was given a cheque for £100 (A most unlikely event) I could take it to the Midland Bank and pay it in to the Bank Clerk (Always a man) who would know me and pass the cheque over a low partition to a ledger clerk (Also a man) who would know the drawer of the cheque and enter it to my ledger account there and then. From that moment I could draw a cheque on that £100. Nowadays it takes four or five working days to clear a cheque through the computer and everything takes longer. Also it seems that some cunning genius in a foreign country could possibly draw on my account in the comfort of his own home, so it is wise to keep the minimum practical working balance in my bank account. It would seem that before long there must be a change of thinking, so as to use more operatives and less high-tech investment while keeping up with efficiency and speed.

My life in the 30s was divided between shop and Church. The shop opened at 8.30am, and I opened it. Closing time was 7pm most days with 8pm on Saturdays, and 1pm on Wednesdays in winter. During the summer there was no half holiday, and my Sunday was taken up by morning and evening services and afternoon Sunday School, which meant that I didn't get all that much sunshine and fresh air. In my case this involved little or no alcohol, ten cigarettes a day, and no sex without marriage. The latter is a principle I have stuck to all my life, but then few women in this world would want to have sex with me in any case, except those who loved me enough to be married to me, so it is nothing to swank about.

My circle of friends just accepted as normal that sex was for the enjoyment of people when they married. There was no TV and the films were firmly censured. Most of us went to the cinema once a week, at least in the winter, and sometimes to a dance at the Spa Ballroom wearing dinner jackets and bowties, but in summer it was nicer to go for a walk or a game of tennis after work. At one time I got a craze for early morning bathing in the sea during the summer. Getting up at 6.30am we cycled down to the foreshore, where we could undress without shocking anybody and jump into the sea in our bathing trunks. Back home, it was wash, shave, and breakfast before 8.30 opening time. But I was too tired before 7pm and couldn't enjoy the evenings, so morning dips were forgotten.

I fell in love while preparing for a concert at St. Sepulchre Street Methodist Church. One character had to wear a crown made of gilded cardboard, and we had to stick 'Jewels' onto it by sucking Rowntrees Clear Gums of many bright colours, and sticking them onto the crown. Some months later I plucked up courage to ask her to go to the pictures with me to see 'Fra Diavolo', a Laurel and Hardy film which I can still remember, and later still I was asking Marjorie's father for his daughter's hand in marriage. By this time, my mother was taking very little responsibility in the business, and with great generosity she left it all to me when we got married, and moved back to Whitehaven to live with her mother and sister.

Married we were in April 1939. The war clouds were gathering, but we didn't care, and our honeymoon was a package deal holiday at Lucerne in Switzerland with Polytechnic Tours. I cannot believe it now, but I think it cost us £14 each, including all meals plus travel by train and ferry. For a further thirty five shillings each (£1-75) we acquired travel vouchers for two full day excursions, two half days, and free trips on the lake steamers as often as we liked. But first we had three days in London at the Bonnington Hotel in Southampton Row, where my Uncle Laurie had asked us to call on him at his office. He was London and South Counties manager for B.T.H. (British Thompson, Houston Co) a firm of heavy electrical engineers, and he was also quite an authority on antique ceramics, in fact I still have a book by him, English Porcelain of the Eighteenth Century by J.L.Dixon (Faber and Faber) price 30s. He took us from his office in the Aldwych, to the nearby Waldorf Hotel where we had coffee in the magnificence of their two-level restaurant. There was a pianist playing at the time, I think, and in recent years I saw a TV programme from that very room, in which Stefan

Grapelli and Oscar Peterson played the most wonderful jazz together.

From the Astoria, Uncle took us to the Caledonian Market, since moved to another site I think, and he looked about among the stalls where he was evidently well known to stallholders. As for me, I spotted a Kodak Colour Film, size 120, at a give-away price, so I went mad and bought one, and later I was the owner of six or eight really first rate 3¼ x 2¼" transparencies of Swiss Mountain scenery.

Then we had an appointment with another Uncle, Mr. Ernest Dixon, who was among the top people in the London Office of the City of New York Bank, in Old Broad Street. There we were allowed to see the vaults, and we went through a huge circular steel vault door, and were automatically weighed as we went in. There in the middle of the floor was a tremendous pile of gold blocks, each so heavy that it needed two hands to lift it. Round the walls were shelves full of bearer bonds, which we were told were worth a lot more than the gold. That day we lunched with Uncle Ernest at the R.A.C. Club in the West End, where we ate in great magnificence, slightly overawed.

The American Ambassador in London used Uncle's Bank at that time, and years before 1939 the then ambassador was a Mr. Kennedy who later became quite famous. I believe Mr. Kennedy was God-father to Uncle's baby girl, my cousin whose name is Heather Kennedy Dixon, who certainly takes a great interest in the Kennedy family.

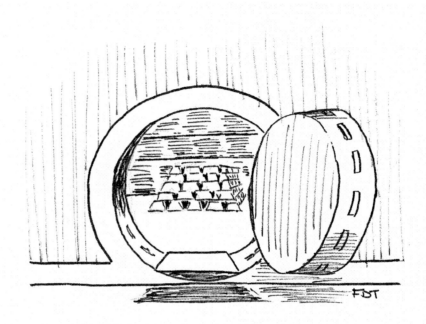

STRONG-ROOM DOOR, CITY OF NEW-
YORK BANK, OLD BROAD STREET
LONDON, 1939.

Uncle Ernest served in the Army in the first World War, in Salonika, and was keen on rifle shooting, being a member of the Bank's team, and I understand won top Bisley prizes. Certainly he had a rifle specially built for him, and a special pair of spectacles like those now used by snooker experts.

Yes, that honeymoon was something to remember. It was April 1939 and, although we were not to know it, by September of that year we would be at war with Germany. When we went to the Rhine Falls, we could see across into

Germany, and for the first time saw the now-famous Swastika on the tender of a railway engine. I walked across a bridge over the Rhine to get a photograph. and at the far side of the bridge was Germany. From the border post on the German side someone shouted at me, and I don't speak German so I finished taking my photo without any sudden movement, slowly turned my back on the German side and walked back into Switzerland with measured tread. Having heard about border incidents, and seeing that the guards were armed, I was more than a little scared.

Our hotel bedroom outside Lucerne was enormous, and contained two big single beds. Single beds on a honeymoon! So I lashed the two beds together using a tie and a pair of braces, and this was fine until the tie broke and the beds drifted apart. In the middle of the night there was an almighty thump, and Marjorie had vanished. Never at my brightest in the middle of the night, I guessed that she had gone to the toilet, but she appeared from the gap between the beds with only a bruise to remind us of it in the morning.

I could write volumes about that holiday, the magnificent scenery, the mountain railways and the steamers on the lakes, but will limit myself to the most scary part of it, for me at least. It was on the boat on the way back from Calais to Dover, in a rough sea. On deck people all round us were being sick and Marjorie felt rotten too, so I took her down to the Ladies Room and left her in charge of a Stewardess as she wanted to go to the toilet. I went back on deck, and watched folk being sick with growing lack of enthusiasm for foreign travel. About half an hour later it dawned on me to go and look for her as she had not turned up, so I searched all the places where cups of tea were being served, and toured all the lounges, but without success. There were three girls on the boat from Scarborough. and they knew Marjorie, so I asked them if they would look round the ladies bunk room. but that drew a blank and together we searched all the public rooms once more. By now I was really worried. and thought how dreadful it would be if I had to return to our new home completely alone. In desperation I revisited the ladies bunk room, and realised that just down a flight of stairs was the men's bunk room. so down I went and found the missing lady rolled up in a blanket fast asleep on a bunk at the foot of the stairs. As I did the 'Prince Charming' act to wake her up, the Tannoy told us that we would be in Dover in twenty minutes. Safe in England and together again. we were two happy people, little knowing that the world would be at war in only four months time.

Back home from the honeymoon. there was a very busy time ahead of us with business and family problems to sort out. Then came registration for National Service, the constant threat of gathering war clouds as Hitler's army marched into one country after another, though my 'Call-up' papers were deferred because I had joined the Special Constables some time before. At that time I ran the shop with my wife during the day, and did guard duty with the 'Specials' most nights. There were times when I Just fell asleep at my desk. Then one day at 11am I was guarding a railway bridge known locally as 'Five Arches' because the IRA were then apt to blow bridges up, when a lady came across the road from a house to tell me that the Prime Minister had just spoken on the wireless, (There was no TV of course) and announced that we were now at war with Germany. From that moment fear was present in every street of every town. The Specials were shown how to extinguish Fire-bombs and to recognise poison gas smells, everyone had to have their gas masks with them every time they went out, and we had tin-hats issued.

Yes, the IRA was a threat even in those days. One night when I reported for duty at the Electric Generating Station (Since closed) the Regular Police told us that three youths with Irish accents had been asking a passer-by how to get to the Electric Light Works. The passer-by told the Police, and we were on full alert, with truncheon, whistle, flashlight and gas-mask as we went out into the complete darkness of the black-out to patrol the grounds.

There was no barbed wire perimeter fence, but behind the works on rising ground there were lots of allotments, each with its greenhouse and wooden hut. In the early hours of the morning when I was alone up near the allotments, there was a crash of broken glass clearly audible above the whirr of the generators, and I held tight onto my truncheon and flashlight. Then I could actually hear it coming towards me on the narrow path, couldn't see it of course, no moon and pitch black dark. But I knew that path and he didn't, and then we sensed each other's presence and I could hear heavy breathing right in front of me so I raised my truncheon and hoped that I would get in a smart bash in the second after switching on my flash lamp.

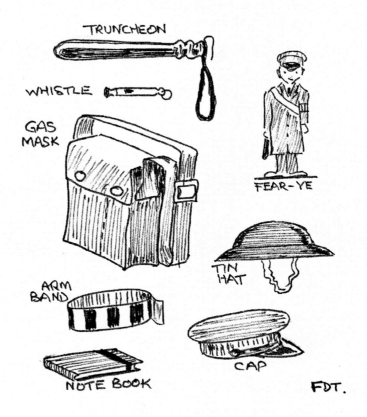

TRUNCHEON

WHISTLE

GAS MASK

FEAR-YE

ARM BAND

TIN HAT

NOTE BOOK

CAP

FDT.

SPECIAL CONSTABLE'S KIT 1939
PLUS A SHILLING OR TWO A YEAR
FOR SHOE-LEATHER AND FLASH-
LAMP BATTERIES

What the light revealed was not a man but a donkey. One of those which before war used to take children for rides on the sands, and which was wondering why this idiot was about to thump him with a stick! I could not arrest a donkey, so I turned it back the way it had come and went to have a very welcome cup of tea from my vacuum flask, and to cheer up the rest of the gang with a bit of comic relief. The IRA did not turn up.

Bombs fell on Scarborough all right, fire bombs in their hundreds, and high explosives too. One night I had stolen an hour or so to go across the road to the Odeon Cinema, when onto the screen was flashed an instruction for all Air Raid personnel to report at once for duty. A 'Land mine' had been dropped in the Old Town near the harbour, and I was sent to a local hospital to help organise traffic, so that the ambulances had clear routes. As one ambulance driver arrived, he said he had an urgent gas case on board, and his patient received immediate attention. There was a sinking feeling in the pit of my stomach because I thought he meant that poison gas had been used, but it turned out later that the casualty was due to town gas (Then lethal) from a gas main fractured by the bomb. In fact casualties were not heavy that night because most people from the Old Town were at a dance some distance away, but many houses vanished completely and broken glass filled the streets.

One night we were woken up by a tremendous explosion which moved our big heavy double bed half way across our large Victorian bedroom. Most nights the siren would wail its warning and we would get into our shelter under the stairs, with the carry-cot containing our baby daughter. Then a public shelter was dug in the garden of the Square opposite our house and shop, and we three regularly moved over there when the sirens warned of a raid. One night the whole town was surrounded by a ring of fires and we received a prolonged delivery of high explosives. Next morning we emerged to be truly amazed to find how much of the town had escaped damage. There were buildings flattened all over the town, and death and injury to be faced and dealt with, but friends were glad to meet you, and you were glad to meet them, because both of you had survived the raid.

It was obvious that I would soon be called up to join the forces, and I wanted to be in the Air Force, so I took a correspondence course in RAF signals theory, and by the time I actually came to put on a uniform it was the light blue one. The great honour of serving as an AC2 was not immediately appreciated by 1485849, Taylor F.D., who was usually referred to as "Sprog" or "Erk" or just "oi you".

The said honour was conferred upon me at Padgate, where I was fitted out and given a number (1485849) which had to be indelibly stamped on my memory, my shoe brushes and everything else which was mine. Each man was also given two fireproof discs which hung on string round his neck, and were also stamped with his personal number. They were hung in such a manner that when you were killed, someone could cut off one disc as a means of identification. One disc was red and the other was green, and you had to wear them even in the bath or at an FFI. We now learned that 'FFI' stood for Freedom From Infection and concerned your state of health regarding syphilis, gonorrhoea, crabs and suchlike afflictions. Three hundred of us were lined up in a very big garage, wearing only a pair of boots. The M.O. and his team went slowly down each line of men, examining those parts that other lagers don't get to. It was cold and there was no wall on the side of the garage we were facing. On the road outside the garage was a constant stream of RAF and WAAF bods who tried their best not to hoot with laughter. I learned two home truths that day, firstly that there is no privacy in the Forces and secondly that I owned the smallest willie in the RAF. Dormice are not well built.

1485849 TAYLOR F.D. "ERK" OR "SPROG"

F/O TAYLOR 149451   CPL TAYLOR

FRANK TAYLOR
CIVILIAN

Before long we were in uniform, except for those who were too tall or fat for standard issue who had to wait the outsize issue they needed. Brass buttons, cap-badge and belt-buckle had to be cleaned for parade every day, as had the boots which had Uskhide soles which did less damage to aircraft than steel studs.

The boots were also kinder to our feet on the parade ground and we soon made our acquaintance with parade grounds and drill Sergeants, to our intense discomfort. One morning we were ordered to pack our kitbags and carry them with our suitcases to Padgate Station. An empty train came in and we got aboard. Everyone wondered where we were going, but all the station names had been completely removed (Information of use to the enemy) and as it was a dull day with no sun, we didn't even know in which direction we were moving, until we recognised York, Darlington and Newcastle and found ourselves decanted onto the station at Whitley Bay to be billeted in semi-detached houses containing only iron bedsteads.

From then on it was drill in the morning, drill in the afternoon and air raids at night. There were some casualties in the raids, but not many, and it helped if you were good at sleeping. Even I could not sleep through the Anti Aircraft fire. The guns sounded to be in our back yards at night, but were completely invisible next morning. Bits of shell would patter down onto roofs, roads and gardens, and all this was known as Ack-Ack. There was an RAF proverb which stated that "What goes up must come down" and we later learned the grim truth of this wry humour.

One day I had my hair cut three times! The Sergeant first suggested it in loud voice about daybreak. "You, get your hair cut". "Yes Sergeant" said I standing smartly to attention and got it cut at lunch time, but asked them not to take too much off, which was a mistake. The Eagle Eye of the Sergeant fell on me almost as soon as I came out of the barber's and I was sent back in at considerable speed. Later that afternoon the full vigour of his highly-coloured language was called into play, and I had to move "At the double" in full kit to the barber for a complete sheep-shearing job, which made it very difficult to keep my so-called Forage Cap on my head, because it was so smooth. Yul Brynner had not been invented then, and dormice feel cold without their fur on, but fortunately it was summer time.

Then there were jabs. Parade outside the MI room at 0800 hours. Queue up for the injections and associated paper work, and back to drill and lectures on the care and use of the SMLE, (Small Magazine Lee Enfield) and the Ross P14 which were the firearms issued to us. Soon we found the odd lad falling flat on the ground as the TAB injections took their toll, and before long we were dragging ourselves back to the billets with 24 hours to get over it. It felt like a bad dose of flu, but did not last as long.

For a couple of days not even the vituperation and invective of the drill sergeant could produce any smartness on the parade ground but gradually we became almost human once more and someone quoted another RAF proverb "Nil bastardo carborundum" translated as "Don't let the bastards grind you down".

In Whitley Bay we ate at a dance hall called The Casino, and it was a constant struggle to get enough to eat. Each or us had a pint-sized pot mug and a steel knife, fork and spoon known as 'Eating irons' which had to be fetched from the billet each mealtime. The tea had lots of sugar in it and it almost made me sick because I hated sugar in tea, having been reared in World War One when sugar was scarce.

YOUR GENUINE WW2 MUG AND "EATING IRONS"

But I had to drink something and that tea was the only thing available. Our pay did not allow for meals after work, I believe that I got three shillings and sixpence a day (17½p) of which I allocated two shillings to my wife and had 7½p a day to spend on riotous living. It would buy a cup of tea at break time if we happened to be near to a canteen, and even a piece of cake at the Church canteen in the evening.

More than once I had to appear before the C.O. The first time was when he saw me sitting with my legs dangling over the back of a motor lorry when we were moving some bedding to a new billet. It was pointed out firmly that :-

This was against the rules

This was dangerous

This practice must cease, forthwith.

On the other hand we could not get into the new billet until Taylor noticed a slightly open first-floor window, climbed up a fall-pipe, got in and opened the front door, and that had gone down a bit better with the authorities. It was certainly the first time I had ever climbed a drainpipe, but they didn't know that.

One evening I was leaving the billet to go to the Church canteen, when I heard a loud and insistent whistle. Looking round, I saw the Sergeant and heard the familiar "OI YOU COME HERE'. I went and stood to attention before the august presence, to hear the single word of command "COOKHOUSE", so my evening was spent peeling a mountain of potatoes which were thrown into a metal dustbin for the next day's lunch. Never again did I respond to a loud whistle, and even that got me into trouble later on, but at Whitley Bay my hands got black from peeling many potato mountains, as I learned the meaning of Fatigues.

There were lectures of all sorts, on rifles, Sten guns. first aid and how to avoid getting venereal diseases. In the latter, the M.O. strongly advised those who must have sex to do so only with professionals, and to avoid at all costs what he called "Enthusiastic Amateurs" who were almost always infected. Fortunately that was no problem for me, as I had only ever had sex with one lady in my life and did not intend to alter that, war or no war. Marjorie and I loved each other very much, and I was, and still am, a Christian. Not a howling success at that, but convinced never-the-less.

Dormice are not all that good at throwing hand-grenades, but I did manage to heave mine far enough out of the trench on the firing range to avoid problems. One poor chap was petrified with fright and having pulled the pin out he dropped the grenade at his feet. The N.C.O. grabbed it and threw it out of the trench with the shout "DUCK"; and duck we certainly did. Fortunately they used five-second fuses for novices, but we all felt deaf after the bang, so I don't think it got far before it exploded.

Better luck attended target practice on the rifle range because I had been used to small-bore rifle shooting at home, and could at least get my rounds on the target without difficulty. Again I was summoned to appear before the C.O., but this time it was to be put in charge of my squad for the passing-out parade, because there were too few N.C.Os. to go round. Three of us were given this unenviable job, and when it was all over the C.O. called us to his office again and complimented us for getting it all right on the day, and yelling out our words of command in a truly 'Airman-like fashion'.

So now I left Whitley Bay for an Ab Initio Wireless Mechanic Course at Glasgow, still in the rank of AC2, or Erk, because the next stage was to attain the status of LAC on completion of training in the trade to which you were aspiring, or so I thought at the time.

CHAPTER 7

Glasgow saw the next part of the RAF saga. Our billets were in a warehouse in Union Street, where fifty of us had two toilets, many blankets with fleas in them, and each also had a rock-hard iron bedstead with three 'Biscuits' of mattress material. Church Canteens were again a real God-send after work, and each day we went to the Royal Technical College in George Street near George Square for lectures and practical work. This was the only course I have known which operated non-stop for the whole 24 hours. There were two 'Shifts', so that half of us had lectures from lpm to 5pm followed by laboratory work from 6pm to midnight, while the other half started with lab. work at lam to 6am and lectures from 7am to noon, and meals were provided at the College. The course covered basic electronic theory and included thermionic valves, as no one had yet invented transistors, let alone Integrated Circuits. As I had already taken a course based on the very text book which we now used, I managed to come out among the top half dozen at the final exam, and we six were told to report for duty as instructors to guide the following intakes through the laboratory work, and given the rank of 'Acting Corporal' (Unpaid), so we could now sew on our stripes and feel very big-headed. I went to a photographer and had my picture taken so that the stripes showed to full advantage.

Work now consisted of eating breakfast at 5pm, working from 6 to midnight, lunch at midnight, and work again from 1am to 6am, with another meal at that time. Twelve hour work and three hours eating time added up to fifteen hours a day, and it was tiring, but we did have Saturday and Sunday off. The six of us were living at an ex-transport 'Hotel' called the Belgrove, in the Gallowgate, which was second only to the Gorbals as a tough area in the City, and we kept ourselves strictly to ourselves, because it was unhealthy to pick a quarrel of any kind with the locals, even if we could understand their powerful accent. But Glasgow folk in general were wonderfully helpful to Servicemen. Often I have got onto a tram (Known as a Carrr-r) and asked the conductor to give me a shout when we got to my stop, and some other passenger would turn round and say "I'm getting off there and I'll get you on your way", and give every help to point me in the right direction.

At this time I used to go to St. John's Methodist Church in Sauchiehall Street where Reverend Brasier Green had a very well attended Church. After evening service there was an informal cup of tea, and we met all sorts of service and civilian folk. There were soloists, and I do remember one lady who had an outstanding voice and who often sang "One fine day" or "Silent Worship", and speaking of fine singing voices takes me back to Paisley.

Two of us, both Methodists, decided to go one day to a meeting at a Methodist Church at Paisley. We found the church, and during the interval I said to my friend (An Irishman by the name of Johnstone) that the four singers sang as though they were members of the Glasgow Orpheus Choir, trained by Sir Hugh Roberton. Our nearest neighbour joined in and said that the singers were indeed members of the Orpheus Choir, and to cut a long story short we later received two tickets to a concert by the Choir at the Saint Andrew Hall. A concert which I will never forget.

One of the budding wireless mechanics in our charge was a violinist in the Scottish National Orchestra and we also got tickets to a concert in the same hall, conducted by Ian White, where I remember that Elgar's Enigma Variations were part of the programme. These two visits to St. Andrew's Hall were tremendous treats in a pretty dull and tiring life. But all things come to an end, and my next 'Posting' was to No.8 Signals School, Cranwell in Lincolnshire, for a sixteen week course on the RAF signals equipment, and again I managed to come out in the top half dozen. Now I was a real Corporal (Paid) and once more was held back by the C.O. to be a Corporal Instructor on one of the airborne VHF Transmitter/Receivers.

It was during this time that I first saw a mysterious aircraft, which sometimes appeared on the grass which served as a runway at the South of the camp. The mystery was 'How the heck does it hope to fly?' because it had no 'Airscrews' or 'Props'. Rumour had it that some chap called Whittle was building it in one of the huge hangers on the South Airfield, and one day it actually taxied up and down the so-called runway making the most amazing high-pitched noise. Because of the noise, and because there was a big hole in the front and at the back, it was known as 'The Vacuum Cleaner'. Next time we heard that engine noise, everyone shot out of the huts to the edge of the airfield, we watched in amazement as the very first British Jet Plane took off for the very first time. History was made, and we did not hear it come back so had it crashed, or what? In fact I believe that it went to another Airfield, but haven't jets come a long way since that day! The Camp Tannoy sent us back to our duties and said that we must on no account mention that aircraft to a living soul outside the camp.

Cranwell was located among many RAF Bomber Command stations, so that when a big bomber raid was building up, the air seemed to throb with the hundreds of aircraft overhead, carrying full fuel tanks and bomb loads, groaning through the air in squadron formation and heading out for Germany on course for 'Target for Tonight'. Some of those raids involved a thousand bombers in one night.

Down on the ground, life was certainly better than Glasgow. The NAAFI was always available, with 'Char and a wad' (Tea and chunk of cake) and even coffee or cocoa, at one or two pence a cup, and at night the bar was well stocked if you could afford it, but there was little heavy drinking. There were film shows at the Camp Cinema and occasional trips to the Pictures in Grantham or Lincoln. The Camp Cinema was great fun. Every night there was a good old-fashioned Western in addition to the main feature and newsreel, and the comment from the audience made even the most corny Western into a riot of hisses, boos and cheers. One night we were all in place ready for the show, when the C.O. arrived with his entourage of officers. Group Captain Probyn was revered by one and all, the Big White Chief himself, he took off his magnificent greatcoat and cap with scrambled egg round the brim, and surveyed the 1,000 strong audience of Airmen, great and small before assuming his seat on the front row. As the house lights slowly dimmed, a loud voice from the back said in solemn Yorkshire tones 'You can sit down now, we've all seen yer" and the roof nearly came off the Cinema.

Part of the training at Cranwell was Morse instruction and we had to build up our speed until we could send and receive at a pretty nifty rate of knots. This process was hard on the nerves and those who just could not succeed had to be 'Re-coursed' or removed to another job. Some had to see the M.O. and it was rumoured that on occasion one had to go to the looney bin.

Then you were put into a cubicle between two big loudspeakers which roared aircraft noises at you from both sides, while you donned a pair of old earphones which brought you loud atmospherics and mush and a little piping Morse signal. To pass the test it was necessary to write down the groups of coded jumbled letters and figures, and the 'PL' or plain language signal which followed, which you sorted out (If you were lucky) from all the noise, to get used to the conditions when actually flying. Then you actually flew! Flight training was at West Camp and this meant a mile walk, to be fitted with a parachute and given a crash course, all of five minutes long, on how to use it and another quicky on the only way to exit from a Procter Aircraft if things went a bit wrong. Then a more thorough briefing on the exercise to be carried out that day, which had to be worked through by contacting a ground-based station on a given frequency, once you were airborne.

The Procter was a monoplane with fixed undercart. The pilot sat in front and the WOP sat behind him, facing aft. The canopy was fixed down and we jogged across the grass with an ear-splitting noise which made conversation completely impossible. There were no concrete runways at Cranwell, so we belted up the grass until it dawned on me that I was looking down at Cranwell Camp and we were flying. This was it! Flying for the first time in my life, and a lot to be done in a short time. First the trailing aerial.

Beside me, mounted on the side of the cockpit was a metal wheel about fifteen inches wide, which had the trailing aerial wound round it, and when we were high enough I could release the safety catch and holding onto the knob on the wheel, unwind the wire which then ran out through a hole in the floor, weighted by half a dozen big lead beads tied onto the end.

Had I then let go of the wheel, the aerial would have run out at high speed to the end of its length, and the six lead weights would have shot off the end of the wire and rained down on Cranwell Camp, which was considered a "Danger to Airmen" and I would have been in a lot of trouble when we returned.

The next hurdle was "DF" or Direction Finding with the aid of a loop aerial and two ground-based radio beacons. The pilot had to fly a straight course during this exercise, while the WOP took bearings and worked out where he was. When I had finished all this I tapped the pilot on the

shoulder meaning that I had finished and gave him the
'Thumbs up' sign, but unfortunately he did not understand
this as I had not bellowed in his ear.

After some time he in turn tapped me on the shoulder and
pointed downwards. We were flying over the Lincolnshire

TAYLOR IN THE RAF PROCTOR

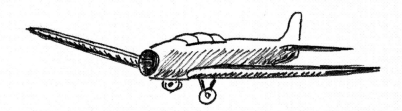

IT HAD NO "PROPS", AND MADE A
NOISE LIKE A HOOVER!
WHITTLE MADE IT AT CRANWELL

coast and heading out towards Germany, so we had a committee meeting which lasted a a full five seconds, and resulted in a unanimous decision to set a course for Cranwell and lunch.

These pilots were often experienced men who were being rested for some reason and yet needed to get flying hours on their personal log books without doing operational duties. One such pilot would ask me to pull in the trailing aerial and then zoom low over a farmhouse, where I guessed his girl friend lived, followed by a couple of tight circles round Lincoln Cathedral which stands on the top of a conical hill. After this he was the model of sobriety and we got on with the exercise of the day.

Another pilot was Polish and had done a full tour of duty in very hazardous operations. He now drove a biplane which the RAF knew as Dominie, and was in civilian life a de Havilland Rapide. As stable a machine as you could find, it had two wings, two engines and a fixed undercart, and would take six lads up at a time. One time when I was transmitting in Morse in this kite, he flew through a thunderstorm and whacking great sparks flew off the aerial winch wheel by my side. Fortunately they missed me. He had his own special way of having fun in a Dominie. At the end of the flight he would return to Cranwel1 at around 7,000 feet and over the Camp would put the nose of the aircraft straight down and pullout into tight vertical turns to port. When speed flagged, he put the nose down again and did turns to starboard, and standing on the grass below this was fascinating to watch. However, sitting in the plane and operating a Morse key, the effect was quite dramatic. The bottom dropped out of my world and I thought "This is it, we've lost control -- wait for the bump". Next moment I was transmitting a continuous Dash, being physically unable to lift my hand or arm which now weighed a ton, and my cheeks began to sag like a bloodhound with the increased G force. Looking out of the window on one side there was a surprising vertical view of Cranwell going slowly round and round. Looking out at the other side there was nothing but clouds revolving the other way round. Not a pretty sight and soon the whole world seemed to go misty and unreal. This was called "Greying out" due to blood rushing away from the head, and since that time I have had an even greater respect for pilots who give aerobatic displays.

It was on one of those exercises that we were flying in and out of the most gorgeous white clouds. As we approached yet one more brilliantly lit wall of cloud, three Halifaxes came out of it flying in the opposite direction barely fifty feet above us! As near misses go that was a beauty, but things were not as highly organised then as they are now. We just took off, flew about, avoiding certain areas, and came back if we didn't hit anything. Me, I didn't say much but I did not trust aircraft all that much, preferring ships as a means of transport, though even ships were not all that healthy to be in during a war.

At Cranwell I first became known as Dormouse. The small group of Corporal Instructors at No.8 Signal School included John Hedley, who later held a top position with Anglo American Oil & Mining in Zimbabwe and it was he who first gave me the nickname of Dormouse because I could sleep through almost any noise.

FLYING DORMOUSE

The hut in which we slept was near one end of the South Airfield and it often happened that Halifax and Wellington bombers were taking off over our heads all night long, doing "Circuits and Bumps" as they practised landing and taking off without pause. Above each bed was a shelf which held a pint-sized pot mug with the aforementioned Eating Irons in it. The whole hut throbbed with the noise of the planes, and the irons jingled about in the mugs. Sometimes the mug would drop off the shelf, so it was safer to move it during "Night flying practice". Cpl. Taylor slept through it all, even when those who had a pint or two on Saturday nights returned, singing and unsteady, it didn't seem to disturb him, hence the nickname.

One evening a group of us were sitting in the NAAFI after work and comparing notes. Among them was Cpl. Peter Sallis, later to become famous as Clegg in "Last of the Summer Wine", and if my memory is correct it was he who pointed out that the latest intake of the Signal School was a class of young Officers. I can almost hear his now well-known voice offering the suggestion "If we are good enough to teach young officers, then we are good enough to be young officers". After due time for deep thought and another mouthful of cocoa or beer, it was decided that some of us would apply for commissions, and we did so immediately.

In due course we were all summoned to Air Ministry in London for an interview. We appeared before a group of five or six terrifyingly Senior Officers, and when my turn came I marched in and flung up a smart salute, and was told to sit down. As question followed question I noticed one Terribly Senior Officer had a pair of folding spectacles. Several times he took them off, folded them at the bridge and also half-way down the side pieces, and put them in a neat arrangement before him on the table. Eventually he spoke. "I see by your medical records, Taylor, that you have one good eye and one poor eye, so why don't you wear a monocle ?" It was obvious that he could have worn a monocle himself, but I risked all and replied "I have worn a monocle in amateur theatricals, Sir, and find it very difficult to keep it in place; and when I do succeed I look very foolish". I swear that one of the other Officers exploded with a chuckle, which he deftly turned into a cough, and I was allowed to stand, replace my cap, and having taken a pace to the rear, salute again and go back to the waiting room fearing that I had probably ended my chances of promotion if the folding-spectacle man did actually wear a monocle.

But we all got through. Eventually we all received orders to go to Cosford for Officer Training, and we packed our bags once more. I had taken my old battered Sunbeam bike to Cranwell, and even though it was on its last legs I hated to lose it when I just had to leave it to rust, as I had no chance to take it to Cosford, or to return it to my home. So it was that Corporals John Hedley, Chuffy Simmons, Dormouse Taylor and others left Cranwell to be young officers.

When we arrived at Cosford, they did not know that we were coming. It was proverbial in the RAF at that time that no one ever knew that you were coming when you arrived at a new station. There were about thirty of us lined up in front of the Admin building, while they made up their minds what to do with us. At long last there emerged from the Admin block a Flight Sergeant who was more or less square with a leg at each corner and wide square shoulders supporting a bull neck and a red face. He regarded us sternly and announced "You're on a Battle Course", explaining that our unexpected arrival had made it impossible for us to go on to officer training immediately. Now a Battle Course was mostly physical exertion, jumping into rivers, climbing ropes and steep cliffs and banging away dummy rounds of ammo. at the enemy amid explosions of all sizes, and we were completely out of form physically, so we did not regard the idea with wild enthusiasm. On the other hand we were in a sense on trial, and if we were to remain as possible Officer material we had to give practical evidence that we could cope with difficult situations. Rumour had it that five percent of entrants on this course normally ended up in hospital, and that they didn't really mind as long as it didn't get up to ten percent. Certainly there were one or two casualties, and most of us had blisters and bruises, but eventually it was all over and we became Officer Cadets, with black and white chess-board bands round our caps. Dormice are not all that good on Battle Courses, and not any great shakes as outstanding 'Leaders of men' on Officer Cadet Courses, but our technical qualifications in our various RAF trades (Wireless Mech. Radar Mech. etc.) stood us all in good stead and gave us a good chance of success.

Actually I remember little of the process of becoming an 'Officer and Gentleman', except that I now had sheets on my bed instead of just hairy blankets, and a much more attractive uniform, paid for out of a special Uniform Allowance. From now on it was First Class Rail travel warrants, which helped me to sleep more comfortably on long journeys, the first of which was to return home and spend a short leave with my family.

My first posting on taking the King's Commission was to No.16 M.U. at Hartlebury near Kidderminster, and here I was to be a Pilot Officer under Flight Lieutenant Mann, one of the best superiors I ever served under. He had come into the RAF as a boy entrant and had won promotion during peace-time when promotion had to be won on sheer merit. He knew more about King's rules and regulations than anyone else on the station, and carried the badge of Aircrew Observer on his uniform. Serving under Flt/Lt Mann taught me a lot of extremely useful things. He could be a hard critic of the work he gave me to do, which brought me down to earth with a thump when I might have got big-headed. He had a dry determined sense of humour, and sometimes with a grin that showed a row of teeth would say "That's you, Taylor, everything in motion, nothing under control", or to himself "When thought of, make a note of" and again "Safe bind, safe find" which meant that if I filed a document in the correct place, I would save a lot of time looking for it later. But he was the world's best friend when you were in a jam, because he would prove you were in the right by quoting chapter and verse from the Rule Book.

Hartlebury was one huge warehouse, with stores of many types held in Hangers each in the charge of Equipment Officers. The Signals Block was a small building with the only windows high up near the ceiling. It housed a room full of teleprinters, a wireless transmitter/receiver and the station telephone exchange, all of which were manned on a 24 hour watch system. The teleprinter and telephone operators were civilian and the Wireless Operators were RAF. Signals were arriving all the time, ordering equipment of all kinds, and a motor cycle despatch rider ran a constant route round the hangers delivering signals to stores sites many of which were some miles away. At one end of the Signals Block was the office of Flt/Lt Mann and P/O Taylor and nearby was the Cypher Office where coded signals were dealt with by the Cypher Queens. These were three WAAF Officers who worked in a locked room of which I never saw the interior, and were seldom seen from one week to the next except at meal times in the Mess. Mann and Mouse were far too busy to worry about Cypher Queens anyway. Both of us were married and old by RAF standards, and our days were very full. Besides the Signals Block we had to supervise the technical side of the enormous stock of signals equipment on a nearby site, organise work on modifications which never stopped as new 'Mods' came through to improve performance in all sorts of ways. Then there was a large Transmitting Site with a forest of aerials for transmitting to the Near East and Far East, and a big secret underground storage site some miles away. We had to turn up at the Signals Block at four or five in the morning to check that the place was properly manned by people who were or their toes, and this was not a popular job with us or with the operators.

Part of the time, I was billeted in an empty vicarage at Elmley Lovett, with a batman between six of us, and a bicycle for transport. Then I was moved to a house in

Hartlebury which was owned by a lady whose husband was a Squadron Leader. When they went away for a few weeks, she suggested that I ask my wife to bring our baby girl to stay, which she did. After only three days the little mite was so ill I asked the Station Medical Officer to have a look at her, and he immediately diagnosed Rubella. The Cypher Queens heard about this in the Mess and one of them, called Pacey, came round to help Marjorie my wife whenever she was off duty. She was a Godsend to us and kept Marjorie going under difficult conditions, in a place where she knew no one, and I shall always be grateful to her. We had to contact the owner of the house, of course, and apologise for bringing the infection, and as soon as little Elizabeth was well enough they both went back home, so they did not see much of Worcestershire.

After six months duty, a Pilot Officer automatically moved up to Flying Officer, and soon after that I was given the job of Mess Officer by the C.O. as no junior Officer escaped extra duties of one sort an another, and I was about the only chap around who did not drink. I was responsible for the day to day running of the Bar from that time, so I had to check the Bar stock from time to time and also check new stock arriving and try to prevent losses of any kind. I did smoke, of course, though not outdoors as Officers were not allowed to smoke or carry parcels when outside. At the next Mess Meeting the C.O. announced with great gravity that "Since Taylor took the job over, the profits on drinks at the bar had improved a lot, but the profits on tobaccos have fallen".

There were a good few pints put away on some nights, but as a rule we were a reasonably well-behaved bunch, with a hard days work to do next day and a pretty grim war going on. In June 1940 Dunkirk saw our defeated army evacuated from Europe, leaving all their equipment in enemy hands or destroyed. Italy joined the Germans, and huge bombing raids were suffered by London, Coventry and Bristol. In 1941 the Russian Government had to leave Moscow under attack by the German Forces, and Rommel was beating us on the North African front. The Japanese attacked Pearl Harbour. On Christmas night 1941 I was Duty Officer, being the only one likely to be stone cold sober anyway, and there was not a lot to cheer me up as far as the war was concerned.

Mind you, there were noisy nights in the Mess sometimes, and from my Office in the HO Building that Christmas night I could hear the powerful sounds of Doc's trumpet. When suitably fortified on special occasions of this sort, our M.O, or 'Doc' as he was known, would sound bugle calls on his trumpet to summon the gang, and a procession would follow him jangling trays and anything that would make a noise, singing at the top of their voices :-

> The bells of Hell go ting-a ling-a-ling
>> For you but not for me.
> The angels they will sing-a-ling-a-ling
>> For all eternity.

Out of the front door of the Mess they would go (As long as the C.O. was not around) round the outside of the Mess building, and back in again at the front. Between the choruses the leader would yell "Sister Anna will carry the banner' at which a WAAF voice from the rear would complain "But I carried the banner last week" and the voice of the leader again "Then you'll carry the bugger again" followed by more trumpet calls and another verse of the Bells of Hell. Then from the rear came in rapid succession the complaints:

> Sister Anna's in my way
> Sister Anna's in everyone's way
> Sister Anna's in the family way

with another musical session to follow. When Doc got really full of enthusiasm he would climb up a fall pipe by the front door, scramble right up over the roof, and down a pipe at the back of the Mess to loud cheers and prolonged applause.

While there I had to go into Kidderminster to visit a dentist and noticed a Victorian-looking office in the centre of the town with a gold-leaf inscription on each darkened window:-

> Doolittle & Dally
> Accountants.

For all I know the firm is still trading under the same delightful style, as friends have assured me quite recently that they are still in business.

It was in Kidderminster that I met again, quite by chance, John Hedley who was such a great help to me at Cranwell. He had been posted to a special unit and we went for a walk together while he explained what was going on. We could not talk in a Pub or Cafe in case we were overheard. Everywhere there were notices "Careless talk costs lives" and we knew how true it was. The German Air Force transmitted a narrow directional beam of wireless signal which passed over their intended target for that night's operations. The bombers flew down the beam until they picked up a second beam at right angles to the first, right over the target, and then they off-loaded their bombs and went home. This was nicknamed by us "Headache".

But our boffins had found a way of receiving the beam signal and re-broadcasting it from a location miles away on the same frequency, so that the beam appeared to the Luftwaffe to bend, and they dropped their bombs on the countryside. This was code-named "Aspirin" and was naturally extremely Hush Hush. It was very effective, but meant great mobility on the part of the teams in the field, and constant vigilance as the narrow beam might appear anywhere at any time.

Pre-war there were Ice-cream sellers on tricycles, called "Stop-me-and-buy-one", which appeared at any place where the public might gather. During the war some RAF stations had one of these and when there was little or no flying taking place the Ice-cream trike would wander slowly around the perimeter track.

But he had no ice-cream aboard, and in its place he had an Aircraft-type transmitter/receiver, and he was in touch with the control tower, imitating the transmissions of dozens of aircraft taking off and landing, for the benefit of enemy listeners who were constantly monitoring every signal we sent. It sounded as though the station was working at full capability, though the aircrew were all on leave and the aircraft being serviced. This was known as "Foxing the enemy".

YOUR GENUINE
"STOP-ME-AND-BUY-ONE'

Also there were "K Sites" which were a full set of airfield runway lights, laid out to convince enemy bombers that there was an airfield below with lights switched on for landing. There was one away out in the country near us, but I never got the chance to see it, and running it was not a popular job, because it could be distinctly unhealthy sitting in a trench after running up the generators and switching the lights on.

One lunch time in the Mess, the Station C.O. asked me if my hearing was failing. He said he had whistled at me across the parade ground, and I had taken no notice at all. So I apologised and told him what had happened at Whitley Bay, and how I had ended up in the cookhouse on fatigues, and I had not looked round from that time if anybody whistled, just in case. Actually I had not heard anyone whistle, and it must have been someone else, because I had not been near the parade ground all morning. It must be understood that C.O.s do not make mistakes, so it was automatically my place to apologise. Not long after that I was told by the C.O. to plant a semi-circle of trees in the garden outside the Mess. I know nothing about trees, but started to search out suppliers of suitable saplings, but fortunately I was posted to London before any progress could be made.

From men who had returned from service overseas, I had heard that one particular transmitter was arriving overseas mangled up and useless because of the design of the 'Cases, transit' in which it was sent from Hartlebury. So I wrote a report to Group R.O. with a suggested design to provide more support where the heavy main transformers were located, and other essential improvements. These boxes had to be six feet high and very tough, as the transmitters were mighty powerful animals as big as wardrobes.

That was not the smartest thing I ever did! A very posh voice from Group R.O. rang me to advise me that a high-powered committee of Top Brass had sat for some time designing the box I had been criticising, and that someone up at Command M.O. was not pleased. Soon after that I had another telephone call from Flt/Lt Jenkins of Air Ministry, Dept S.M.11 (Signals, Maintenance) to tell me to report to him for "A very interesting job", and that I would like the job, but I might not like the place that I was going to do it! So I had to go to the Adjutant's office to find that the thing was all there in writing, and to get my Clearance certificate. This I had to take to lots of offices all over the camp, and each signed that I did not owe any money or have any other uncompleted responsibilities, and I only just got it all done before I had to shoot off to London. My packing had to be done overnight, and after grabbing a few hours sleep, and having an early call from the duty telephonist, I headed for a Transit Mess in Endsleigh Gardens, not far from Euston Station, and found the office of Flt/Lt Jenkins in Woburn House, Southampton Row. He turned out to be a man who knew what he was doing, and did it with great attention to every detail, and with concern for those working under him. I had many reasons to be grateful to him for the rest of my service career. The telephone number of Woburn House was then three letters, followed by 4411, a number I have seen used by the B.B.C. for phone-in programmes and I wonder if they use the same building, but I recently drove up and down Southampton Row looking for Woburn House without success.

It was explained to me that the RAF wanted to set up a Crystal Unit to adjust the frequencies of Radio Crystals, in the Far East. It was to comprise an F/O (me) and six N.C.Os, and be attached to the Headquarters of BAFSEA at Delhi, though we would be responsible to S.M.11 in London direct. First we had to have some months training in the processes of grinding and etching crystals, then go overseas to adjust the frequencies of radio crystals as required in Delhi. I call them Radio Crystals, but we still referred to them as wireless crystals at the time, they are little bits of quartz about half and inch square and very thin. These slices of crystal vibrate at a natural frequency which depends on their physical dimensions, and they can be made to vibrate at a very precise frequency by electrical means, to be used to ensure that transmitters and receivers operate at exactly the right frequency and wavelength.

Now began a fascinating period when I was sent for a few days or weeks to a succession of places to learn about crystals and their treatment and manufacture. I went to RAE Farnborough, which is a research establishment (Or was at that time) where truly amazing things were happening, all very secret, and where extremely advanced academics tried their best to educate me in the properties of quartz and its limitations in use. There was a visit to Illminster, to an STC factory which was actually making crystals for use in the services, and a time at Dollis Hill where I learned from the Post Office Research Establishment, and saw their quartz crystal clock, then the most accurate clock in the world, and which they had made themselves. This last was a weeks course for men and women from all three services, all of whom were to work with crystals in some way. A week at an American Station near Cheltenham introduced me to the crystal grinding machines we were to be using, but of course our destination was a close secret which not even N.C.O.s were to know about, and I could not tell my family.

A further week was spent at a factory at Workington in Cumberland (No, not Cumbria) where all seven of us were taught to etch crystals down to a precise finish in a powerful chemical, ammonium bifluoride. Seven miles away from Workington, my mother lived in Whitehaven, at 2 Laurel Bank, so Marjorie brought little Elizabeth over and we all stayed with 'Gran' for a very happy week, while I went by bus to Workington each day to learn my trade. The final day of that week was the last day the crystal team was to be together until we joined up again at our destination, and started to set up shop. So the lads tried a joke on me. They actually helped me into my greatcoat, which I should have known was strange, but I little knew that they had persuaded the blondest blonde in the factory to comb out as much hair as she could spare, and had draped it round the back of my coat as they helped me put it on. Luckily for me and unluckily for them, it blew off before I got back to Marjorie, or I would have had difficult explanations!

During that time at Air Ministry the enemy was sending over a steady stream of Buzz Bombs, the V1 unmanned aircraft or flying bomb. They flew quite low, with a peculiar rattle-roar which one soon learned to know, and they were quite safe until that noise stopped. Then they simply fell out of the sky and went bang. A lot of damage and a lot of casualties resulted and if you heard one go silent, you dived for cover and waited hopefully. In the train on the way to Illminster, one of these nasty things flew alongside the train for a little while as it overtook us, and we were mighty glad when a curve in the line took it out of range. because they tended to veer to one side or the other as they came to ground. For some time I was staying with my Uncle Ernest in Norbury, and quite a few of them came down near us then. Many nights I spent in the Air raid shelter at the bottom of the garden, and sleepless nights don't help dormice much.

One morning at Woburn House they told me that "Another gas-main exploded early this morning" and when I innocently asked why so many gas-mains were exploding, they patiently explained as to a small child that this was a euphemism for Hitler's new weapon, the V2 rocket bomb. Soon after that the whole building shook to a loud crash which seemed to be followed by the sound of thunder tapering off to silence. That was it. The V2 travelled above the speed of sound as it came down, and the roar of the rocket didn't arrive until after the bomb hit. It might seem as though life was extremely risky, and indeed it was during a heavy bombing raid, but the worst raid I heard of caused 3,000 casualties in one night, and twice that number are killed on the roads of this country every year and I bet you still travel about every day in spite of that. So did Londoners, who I admired, go about their day-to-day living in spite of indiscriminate bombing, and sad to say we and the Yanks did a good deal of blanket bombing ourselves so we couldn't blame the other side. OK perhaps they did it first, but two wrongs.........

My musical education was broadened further when I was given a ticket to a concert by Yehudi Menuhin, at the Albert Hall, and with two others from Endsleigh Gradens I found myself in a box in that famous building listening to the Maestro in spite of wars and bombs and blackouts. A glimpse into another world of peace and tranquillity which I will never forget.

CHAPTER 8

Some time in 1943 I think it was, that I was posted to a Transit Centre in Blackpool, with a week of embarkation leave first. Leaving Marjorie on that occasion was not easy, neither of us knew whether we would ever see each other again, and as the train pulled out of Scarborough Station I was gulping pretty hard. The sirens had gone for a red alert before the train pulled out, and Marjorie had a narrow escape on the way back to her parents house at 78 Scalby Road. She actually saw the bombs leave the low-flying aircraft as she crossed Wykeham Street Bridge, and they hit the next bridge, about 200 yards away. Luckily I knew nothing about this as I headed for Blackpool, but she arrived at her mother's home pretty shaken, poor thing.

First we had to draw from stores (Woolworth's closed for the duration) our Tropical Kit. This consisted of khaki drill shorts and long trousers, and jackets to match with huge brass buttons plus a dreadful topee hat. They all looked like the Boer War gear, drainpipe trousers, shorts below the knee, and the hat was so absurd that we fell about laughing. A separate journey to Woolworth's was needed for the bedroll, as it weighed half a hundredweight, and we had to hump it to our billets. It seemed that "Officers will not carry parcels outdoors" didn't reach as far north as Blackpool, because you could see them carrying stuff about all day long. Yes, I know, "There's a War on ".

Each day we reported to the Red Lion Hotel on the Promenade. It was closed, and was being used as Administration offices, so lists were posted every day showing names of those who had to have Jabs, or were due to embark. There were quite a few injections, of which one (I think it was Blackwater fever) came straight out of the fridge and was like being bitten by a snake. I had a painful ear infection, and needed treatment at the MI Room for that as well.

My room mates persuaded me rather against my will to go to the Winter Gardens to a performance of the ballet Copelia. I had never seen a ballet 'Live' and of course TV had not been invented, but I certainly enjoyed that show enormously. Again there was the experience of being in another world for a couple of hours, but this time we returned to a Blackpool free of bombs and rockets, to await the risks of mines and submarines at sea. Quite a different psychological climate, with everybody appearing to be humorously confident, while inwardly doubting newspaper reports and wondering just how bad things really were.

The last thing I remember about Blackpool was leaving Blackpool South railway station, complete with luggage, bed-roll, revolver and briefcase containing my accumulated knowledge of quartz crystals and their habits. The train arrived at Liverpool quay, within sight of the Royal Liver Building, and we walked down to the quay to the waiting "Queen of Bermuda" and up the gangplank bound we knew not where. At least I knew my eventual destination, but nothing else. One lad walked from the top of the gangway straight across the ship and was sick over the other side, and that was in a dead calm sea in dock. The cabin I was sent to had four bunks, in two vertical pairs, plus a loo and shower.

F/O TAYLOR 149451 HUMPING BEDROLL AT BLACKPOOL

"OFFICERS MUST NOT CARRY PARCELS"
BUT
"THERE'S A WAR ON, PAL, — HUMP IT"

The shower was supplied with heated sea-water and the ship's shop sold sea-water-soap which was hopeless as far as lather was concerned, but better than no soap at all, and we could keep clean though rather salty.

Leaving the river Mersey, we said "Goodbye" to England and wondered when, if ever, we would get back again and whether recent reports of success in North Africa were propaganda or fact. They just could not publish much information because it all went straight back to the enemy and was immediately denied by German Radio and "Lord Haw-Haw" who was a dissident Briton broadcasting propaganda for the Nazis.

Next day we found ourselves in a convoy, and various opinions were expressed as to whether we were moving slowly North, West or South as it was dull and overcast. One guess was as good as another, but in a couple of days the wind was screaming through the rigging and we were heading into seas which came in over the bows like Niagara falls. During the day time some of us walked up and down the lea side of the deck for fresh air and exercise. The deck tilted so much that we were walking up a steep hill one minute, and down a steep hill the next, as the Queen pitched fore-and-aft. At night I persuaded my room-mates that the ship was hitting the bottom every time the bows went down with the sea. Certainly there was a loud "Thud" each time, and we later realised that this was the noise of the Atlantic bursting up through the holes in the bows where the anchor chain ran.

Most of the thousand or so servicemen and women were seasick, and the whole boat smelt disgusting, which was one reason for those who could do so to get fresh air even in a howling gale. Eventually the wind moderated somewhat, then one night we could see lights in the distance which may have been the coast of Spain as it was not long before we passed the conical Rock of Gibraltar and entered the Mediterranean. Now the Navy escort ships turned about and steamed past us on their way back to England, and we broke convoy and found that as darkness fell the whole ship was lit from stem to stern. We saw Malta in passing, and also the African coast where 'Monty' and the Desert Rats had so recently beaten back Rommel. One day we passed close to a large naval vessel which sent us an Aldis signal. Having taken the Morse course we read that there were mines ahead at a stated location, but the next excitement was entering the Suez Canal at Port Said. Obviously the traffic in the Suez Canal was one way only, and we had to wait near Port Said until the movement was North-to-South. The Queen of Bermuda was surrounded by little boats full of Arabs with things to sell, and as by magic long thin ropes were lowered down from the decks with money for wonderful bargains being offered. Not a few chaps were rather disappointed with their purchases when they pulled the rope in, but it was great fun. Two small boats were pulled aboard complete with their tough-looking crews, and they remained at the sharp end of the ship until we got through the Canal. Rumour had it that if we had to stop, the Arabs would take ropes ashore and fasten land-anchors so that our ship would remain in the centre of the canal and not risk grounding in shallows. Meanwhile they also produced goods for sale and made a few honest shekels as they whiled away the hot sunny day.

Hot and sunny it certainly was, even in December, From the top deck you could look ahead along twenty miles of canal with parallel sides which seemed to almost meet in the distance. But before they met you noticed the curvature of the earth as the lines appeared to rise up, curve over, and dip down over the horizon.

THE SUEZ CANAL DOES SHOW THE
CURVATURE OF THE EARTH, BUT IT
IS NOT EASY TO DRAW IT!

On each side of the Canal was sand. Sand in dunes, sand with palm trees, sand with camels, sand with ruined concrete buildings, but mile after baking mile of sand. Then we were ordered to don our khaki drill uniforms, and at once the whole ship was laughing from one end to the other.

Even the most senior officers were there in shorts below the knee, very long khaki jackets, and those ridiculous topees, parading up and down the deck doubled up with laughter.

This gear must have been made for Kitchener and his lads, and the only thing we lacked was spine-pads which they wore but which had mercifully been discontinued. (Only quite recently we were told).

STANDARD ISSUE TROPICAL KIT 1943 — AT LEAST IT GOT A LAUGH!

Progress was very slow, because the action of our propellers resulted in the water piling up near the bows but shallow near the stern, and we imagined that if we tried to go faster the stern would ground on the bottom.

A CAMEL-CART WOULD CARRY CROPS, FAMILY AND BELONGINGS IN ONE LOAD

Down the west side of the canal was a camel track and at times we passed groups of Egyptians with camels and donkeys. One group of locals we passed had a magical effect on the ship. These lads raised their burnous at the front, and appeared to me to find about a couple of feet of thick rope underneath, which they grabbed and swung round in circles in great glee. Only it wasn't rope, and it was part of themselves, and it was gigantic, and everybody on board dashed across to the starboard side with shrieks from the girls aboard. The Tannoy crackled to life persuaded as many as possible to go back to the port side as the Queen was listing too far to starboard for peace of mind on the bridge. Order was quickly restored as the apparition moved astern and there was nothing to look at but sand.

DANGEROUS "LIST" ON THE SUEZ
DUE TO LOCAL LADS FLASHING

At Ismailia we emerged into the Bitter Lakes, and had to anchor there while local divers went down to inspect the ship's hull. It turned out that we had bumped the stone piers on leaving Liverpool docks, and since then had kept afloat with the aid of a hasty internal concrete patch and a lot of pumping. Good thing we had known nothing about it in the Atlantic storms. More permanent repairs having been completed, we resumed our journey southwards and entered the Red Sea beyond Suez. The sea was not red, but the cliffs certainly were, for many miles we saw red hills in the distance, and I saw red spots all over my chest! Fearing I had caught something which would spread all over the ship, I reported sick, but the MO only laughed at me, and showed me his chest which looked the same as mine.

"Prickly Heat" he said, "And you'll have lots more of it before you get home", so I went back feeling less like a leper and found that the MO was right and most of us were covered with it.

We halted at Aden for a while in intense heat, and a large consignment of Indian currency was put aboard. I was detailed with quite a number of junior officers as acting paymaster. As each man came to my pay-table, the NCO at my side told me how much he was to be paid, and I counted out the Rupee notes, So as the queue got shorter, my stock of notes dwindled. Imagine my surprise when the money worked out exactly right to the last Rupee for the last man. The story we had heard was that we had to make good any shortage ourselves, but I rather think there must have been some contingency provision because we were quite unused to doing this job, and were just chosen at random.

After a few more days watching the circle of the horizon in the Indian Ocean, and listening to lectures on life ashore in India we berthed at Bombay, near the India Gate which looked like a larger version of the Marble Arch. Now there was some action to watch, as they started to unload the ship's holds and the "Not wanted on voyage" suit cases and kit bags went ashore. The dockside looked spotlessly clean by English standards, and the locals looked pretty clean in the sunshine also.

DELHI ARCH AND "SECRETARIAT"

We all began to pack our personal belongings, and I regret to say a lot of discarded tins and bottles were shoved out of portholes on the side of the ship away from the pier. I was very impressed to see eager Indians in little boats on that side, pulling out of the water all these tins and bottles such as Andrews Liver Salts and Talcum Powder empties. That, I said, showed how much better they are at keeping docklands clean and tidy than in Liverpool and London.

It was not until much later that I realised that this eagerness was due to private enterprise rather than public pride. One day I bought, at a small stall in Bombay, a tin of Johnson's Talcum Powder. It was full of flour, and had no doubt been hauled from the dockside out in the sunshine and lovingly refilled, so here was another meaning of the saying 'Caveat emptor' - let the buyer beware. Once ashore, we were piled into RAF lorries, formed into a convoy, and driven through the streets of Bombay to Worli Camp on its Northern outskirts. There was a motorcycle escort ahead and behind the convoy of lorries, and they did a lot of spectacular zooming in and out of the traffic so we realised that speed limits and driving constraints were rather different in India. There were teeming millions everywhere, and every bus and tram was jam-packed full of humanity. We drove passed the beautiful palm trees of the garden standing on a slight hill where the remains of Indians of certain castes are burned or picked clean by vultures. Then for some miles we ran along the seaside promenade with impressive western style buildings. At one stage we were away from the coast and beside a vast man-made trench designed to run-off the worst of the monsoon rains, but at that time bone dry. We were held up for some minutes by the traffic and I saw a steady trickle of people walking from the nearby buildings, cross the road and go and sit down on the banks of the monsoon ditch. Having had lectures aboard the ship to help us to understand the land of Hindu and Moslem religions, I thought that this must be a religious observation as they seemed to spend only a short time deep in thought squatting on the grass before returning across the road. It turned out that there was no constraint as to where they performed nature's functions either. Then we passed an open drain running from city to sea, and we could smell it for miles.

At last we reached the RAF transit centre at Worli and junior officers were "Fell in" at once complete with revolvers and topees. We were marched in powerful heat to the Armoury where we checked in our revolvers and then round to a wire-fenced compound which contained an enormous pile of service sun-hats. "Right, gentlemen, just chuck your hats on the top of that lot" said the NCO in charge, and that was the last we saw of them, thank goodness. We asked ourselves whether someone in England was making these things. while someone in India was setting fire to them, or whether the same hats were returned to the UK for re-issue. No doubt when the war was over it would be re-organised so that Tropical Kit was more suited to tropical life, but there was a war going on and there were problems more pressing than sun-hats.

PILE OF TOPEES AT BOMBAY — DID THEY GO BACK TO UK FOR RE-ISSUE ?

Now we found ourselves in brick-built rooms, each containing about forty Charpoys, with toilet blocks outside where chloride of lime was spread around each day with a generous hand, so they always smelt of chlorine.

OFFICER-SAHIB'S CHARPOY AND
MOSQUITO-NET — DAYTIME

NIGHT-TIME DITTO. MOZZY
NET DOWN, SNORE-SNORE,
BEWARE OF DORMOUSE!

A Charpoy is a low wooden framed bed with string or rush webbing criss-crossing it from side to side. A thin wooden frame above the bed holds up the mosquito net, which has to be tucked in with meticulous care under the thin mattress to prevent the little demons getting at you during the night. It was here that we first met 'Pinky-pani', a solution of potassium permanganate. We were instructed to immerse all fresh fruit or vegetables in this horrid stuff before eating it, and to wash our hands as well. This gave the Indian 'Bearers' a great deal of quiet amusement, doubtless they could see behind the scenes in the cookhouse and knew what did not happen there.

As in Blackpool, so in Bombay, we all went each morning to read the lists of names on the notice board. It seemed a very long wait until one day my name appeared on a list to entrain for Delhi. That night I took a last look around Worli, walked along its beautiful promenade beside the sea, heard again the Indian music coming from the open windows of the music school, and packed up my belongings ready for an early morning 'Wakey-Wakey'. Next morning it was back onto the three-ton lorries piled with men and luggage, and we had another display of wizardry from the motorcycles on our way to Bombay Station. At any given moment it seems that everyone in India is going somewhere else, and going by train. Our train was a troop train, and at least we all had seats, even though they were only slatted wood and uncomfortable, but a glance at the suburban trains bringing workers to the Bombay factories just took our breath away.

Local trains in India are packed with solid humanity to a degree which defies description. The interior of the carriage is just one mass of bodies, like a London Tube at rush hour, the doors are wide open with folk hanging out and clinging on, while others ride on the buffers and couplings between the carriages. Some even manage to get onto the roof in spite of the electric wires over their heads, and we wondered at the discomfort and suffering not to mention the risk which Bombay people would endure to go to work each day. They always appeared to be cleanly, if rather gaudily dressed, and one was often more aware of BO from Europeans then from Indians. Now that was odd in itself, because of the way they seemed to wash clothes. The Dhobi-Wallah did not ever seem to use soap, preferring to swing each garment over his head, soaking wet, and whack it down onto a flat stone. At least that was what we were told, but I think that soap must have figured in the process somewhere, as the khaki drill came back every day looking spotlessly clean. We needed clean bush-shirt and shorts every day, and a bath after work each day also.

VILLAGE SHOPS

However, back on that troop train we chugged along at a gentle rate of knots through a new land of mystery. Village after village came and went, with sand, a few palm trees, and more sand, with some scrubby vegetation under the hot sunshine.

The villages comprised groups of grubby mud huts, stained red near the ground with what we came to know as beetle-nut juice, and usually an area of cultivated ground where whitish cows were slowly pulling wooden ploughs or walking in monotonous circles driving a machine for raising water from the well.   Here and there women walked in stately strides, with metal water-pots on their heads, to and from the wells, but I never saw a man carrying water. I remembered that in one of the Gospels, Jesus told his disciples once to look out for a man carrying a water-pot, and to follow him to his house where they were to prepare the Last Supper. I now realised that it would be very easy to spot a man carrying a water pot in an Eastern country. (Luke 22 v10).

FETCHING WATER IS A WOMAN'S WORK
AND IS OFTEN A LONG HAUL.

Bonny little brown children sat on the ground in the sunshine, making discs like thick pancakes out of cow dung and straw and putting them out in long lines to dry in the sun. These were not used as fertiliser, but as fuel for cooking. Some men were working in the fields, but the majority were doing nothing in particular, which after all was what we were doing, all day, all night, and the next day as well.

At long last we chugged into Delhi, hot, dusty and dirty, and glad to have a charpoy to sleep on in the transit camp, with a bath and a cooked meal in the cool of the evening. It was certainly cool also in the morning, and though I could scarcely believe it there was hoar frost on the grass so we had on our blue uniforms and even greatcoats. This was January of course, and by June we were going to forget that hoar frost could even exist in Delhi.

I had arrived ahead of the six NCOs and the equipment. They had heard of the way things disappeared between dockside and destination, so they had decided quite on their own, to ride shot-gun with our crystal grinding outfit, and they deserved a medal each for that alone, but did not get one! They endured considerable hardship on a very long journey, but not a thing was lost from the cargo en route, so we had a good start to operations.

While I waited for the arrival of the team and equipment, I was attached to the Signals Admin offices of BAFSEA (British Air Force South East Asia) and helped in an office at

Headquarters, where I worked under a very friendly Scot who came from Larkhall in Lanarkshire, and being called J.C.Burns he was naturally known as 'Robbie' by one and all unless senior officers or top brass were around when everyone was on formal terms and surnames and rank were used. Work in that office meant a pile of manila folders, each holding correspondence on some matter, and each requiring a carefully worded letter or memo to be written so that the actual decision to take action was if humanly possible passed on to another department, or at least to a higher authority. We supposed that eventually these files went so high that someone somewhere actually had to decide something, but I always hoped it wasn't me, as dormice are not good at making Big Decisions and I had nothing to rely on except instinct. A dormouse's main instinct is to take aboard a lot of food and go to sleep, but that solved nothing at all.

Only two really useful things did I do there, while waiting for the equipment to arrive from the UK. Pick locks, and look like another member of permanent staff. Indian locks were not that difficult to understand and to unfasten, given a length of galvanised wire and a spot of patience. Having taken a few such locks to pieces, I knew what went on inside, and once or twice I was sent for by very senior officers to open locked boxes or trunks when "The keys had been lost". My second achievement resulted from a visit by Top Brass from London, whose duty it was to reduce staff at BAFSEA. In the RAF, the 'Establishment' of Officers was in the form of a pyramid, so that to appoint a Group Captain there had to be two Wing Commanders. Each 'WingCo' had to have two Squadron Leaders under him and each Squadron Leader needed two Flight Lieutenants, and so on. Therefore if someone declared one very junior officer redundant, it meant that probably the one above him had to go as well, and this ran right up the pyramid to the Head Boy (Who was very senior indeed and didn't intend to be moved). So you can understand why there was much tidying of offices, and all 'In' trays had to be piled high with files, showing how much work there was to be done. Feverish activity was everywhere, with Indian messengers hurrying everywhere at once, until the 'Buzz' went round that 'They' had finally left Delhi, and we got down to the Times of India Crossword, and other serious matters. Apparently my presence looking busy prevented the axe from falling in our neck of the woods.

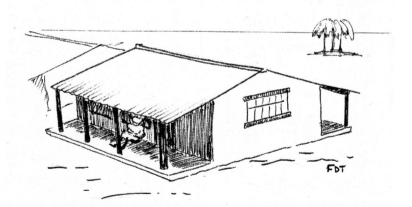

CRYSTAL LABORATORY, INDIA,
AT WILLINGDON CAMP, RAF,
WITH "CHOWKI-DAH" AT THE DOOR

When the Crystal Grinding and Etching equipment did arrive we really got down to hard work, in a brick-built hut, next to the Crystal Store (India) at the end of the runway at Willingdon Airport, which was about three miles from Travancore Mess where I now lived. We set up our laboratory, and from that moment we marked all the crystals which went from it as 'XLI' which stood for Xtal Lab. India, and whenever a crystal was called for which was not in stock, we had to make it.

We had a large bank of quartz slices to work from, so we selected one (or more) which oscillated at a frequency lower than that required, and first we had to slightly reduce its thickness by grinding between two 'Laps', or flat steel wheels about a foot across, by about an inch thick, using our American Lapping Machines. The final process was to bring it exactly up to frequency (Down in size) by etching in Ammonium Bifluoride (Nasty stuff) using a repeated Etch-and-test treatment until we got it bang on. One dip too many in the bath of bifluoride and you were over the top and had to put that blank back into store and start another. Then each crystal was assembled in its outer case, marked with its frequency plus XLI, and given a test over its entire temperature range, from below freezing to 60°C if I remember correctly.

This last test involved a rack of six little ovens which I had to design and have made up locally. Each oven was electrically heated to 70°C and the crystal was placed into it direct from a refrigerator where it had been well down below 0°C, so that it moved from freezing up to at least 60°C and during this time it was connected to a small oscillator circuit which was in turn connected to a recording meter, and the print-out showed very clearly if the crystal stopped

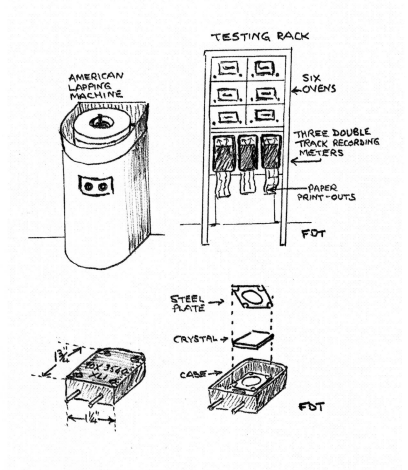

RAF CRYSTALS AROUND 1944

oscillating anywhere over the temperature range. If this happened, we had to give it a treatment called "Edging" which reduced one of its lateral dimensions, as the usual cause of the fault was spurious oscillations in longitudinal mode, which interfered with those of the intended 'Shear' mode of mechanical vibration.

To do all this we had to have some other oscillator of reliable accuracy with which to compare our crystals. We had one very stable crystal which lived in a temperature-controlled space for the whole 24 hours and its oscillations were constant to within a few parts in a million, but this could be adjusted very slightly to bring it absolutely into agreement with a yet more reliable standard crystal oscillating away somewhere in the BBC back in England. The BBC crystal was used to control precisely the frequency of a certain transmission which we could actually receive in Delhi. We put up four wooden poles, and designed an aerial which we pointed hopefully towards England, dug out a good deep hole for an earth rod, and it worked!

Our HRO receivers (American again) brought in the required transmission after one of our men who was a Radio Ham had tried for some time, and sitting in a hut in India we had a reliable reference for the whole of our work, to which we could tune at favourable times each 24 hours and correct our secondary standard crystal against the BBC by using an oscilloscope until it was well within one part in ten million. Also part of the transmission was modulated at one kilohertz so we could also correct out audio oscillators at the same time. Incidentally, we could also hear the BBC World Service which made us feel very much nearer home and kept us up to date with current affairs, or at least with current propaganda. Not only that, but we could tune to Japanese propaganda and a wonderful little Japanese girl singer, whose theme-tune 'Rose-Rose' was on everybody's mind for years.

Each of the frequency comparators with which the team worked was corrected against our secondary standard crystal. Using circuits which produced a vast range of harmonics and sub-harmonics, plus others which gave us steps of 50 and 10 KHz (Kilohertz) with a final audio oscillator in Hertz (Then called 'Cycles-per-second') so that we could locate a crystal onto the precise frequency called for, to 50Hz which was well within Air Ministry specification DCD WT 914.

But this was work which needed concentration, careful calculation, and a lot of patience, which was not easy in a temperature of 100°F which could even reach 120°F on a bad day. Sweat just rolled off our eyebrows and nose-ends, our khaki Bush-shirts had huge black patches of sweat on them most of the time despite the ceiling fans, and we needed a bath every night before evening meal.

Talking of baths brings to mind my palatial 'Go-down' at Travancore Mess, once the Delhi home of the Maharajah of Travencore, located near the impressive Arch (Like the Arc de Triomphe) about a mile down the flat grass-lined road which started at the Secretariat Building. But my bath was rather less majestic. A tin tub, with a cold water tap sticking out of the brick wall about eighteen inches.

TEPID BATH BEFORE
EVENING MEAL

Each officer had a 'Bearer' or personal servant, who brought
in a couple of buckets of hot water when his 'Sahib' arrived,
and cold water was added as required. Too hot, and you
sweated bucketfuls. Too cold, and you could get a chill.
Tepid was ideal. Every night after the bath you needed a
newly washed and ironed set of KD (Khaki Drill) so a stock
of these had to be built up. On the camp was a Durzi-
Wallah, or tailor, with a dozen or more Indians sitting on the
sandy floor with sewing machines. The Durzi would
measure and make a few notes which looked like spider-
webs on a piece of paper, and you called next day, paid
cash, and took away your new uniform. It fitted perfectly.
And it cost next to nothing.

The day started with breakfast in the Mess Dining Hall at
07.30. Each officer had his bearer, who brought his food

and refilled the tea-cup. The bearers all wore standard uniforms in immaculate white, with wide belts and turban head-dresses which had starched fan-shaped cockades sticking up from one side, most impressive. Then a cycle ride of about three miles took me to the laboratory for 9am opening. On one side of the camp was a monsoon ditch, which must have been between forty and fifty feet deep, dry for most of the year, but which carried away some of the water when the rains carne. Work started at once, with no time for crosswords or newspapers. All the same, we had a lot of fun doing the daily chores, and the electric fans helped to keep us reasonably comfortable. But we welcomed the arrival of the Char-Wallah in the middle of the morning.

"CHAR-WALLAH", A WELCOME VISITOR TO THE LAB. TWICE A DAY.

Whether he was an official, or self-employed, I never found out, but he had a pole across his shoulders with a heavy load on each end which he set down in the shade of our wooden verandah. One end consisted of a tin trunk which opened to reveal cakes and buns of all kinds, and at the other end was something like a milk churn in steel and copper with a charcoal fire burning underneath it to keep the 'Char' (Tea) 'Bart gurrum' (Very hot). Cups of tea were only a few Annas, and nothing cools you like a hot cup of tea when it is really hot down South.

Lunch time took one of two forms, either I could cycle back to Travancore Mess and back, doing my 'Mad dogs and Englishmen' act, or if it got too hot for that I could get a lift on a lorry to another Mess which was nearer to the laboratory, but was very formal and not too friendly.

After lunch, more work on the crystals, plus the interminable administrative paper work, until we finally locked the doors about six o'clock and cycled back to bath and evening meal, and then a number of Nimbu-panis during the evening. The Nimbu or Nimboo was a citrus fruit like a lemon, which was squeezed and sweetened to form a delicious cool drink. One night I remember drinking eight big glasses of the stuff, and I don't think I drank anything stronger than that during my stay in India. In the hot weather we were far too exhausted to do much after work, but at other times I was persuaded to help with stage lighting for an RAF presentation of Androcles and the Lion, which was a huge success in spite of my efforts.

That stage lighting job resulted in a trip for me to Calcutta, about 800 miles away by air. This is how it happened. We needed about 50 yards of thick cab-tyre flex, and there was none in any place which was accessible to us in Delhi, but the CTO (Chief Technical Officer) located some in Calcutta which he could call upon. The question was - How to get it from Calcutta to Delhi – and that question was answered in a typical RAF way. The Americans had a Crystal Unit in Calcutta, so it became a matter of urgency that I should visit that Unit for technical reasons (Unspecified) as we were using the same grinding machines as they employed, and needed advice. So I left the Laboratory in charge of the senior Sergeant and one dark night I boarded a Dakota of the RAF which rattled through the Indian night for hour after hour, to land at Dumdum Airport in the dawn light, and I mustn't forget while in Calcutta to pick up the cab-tyre flex!

The King George Vth Hotel, facing the maidan or park, was possibly the best in Calcutta, but was now full of Officers of all Services. Crammed full. I was given a bed in a huge room which held four other chaps and the beds were so well separated that there was room for two or three large easy chairs and lots of space even then, but having caught a streaming cold I had a good hot bath and retired under my mosquito net to sleep it off. Someone woke me up to ask if there was a Flt/Lt Smith in that room. I said that there was, but that he had gone out with the rest of the chaps. It appeared that a WREN officer who said she was his sister was asking for him and could she wait in the dormitory until he returned. I said certainly, if that was what she wanted to do, and had time to see a fluffy blonde in Naval uniform, before turning over and going straight to sleep.

I never woke up when the others returned, so I still have no idea what happened after that, and I didn't ask. Only later did I realise that I had spent at least part of the night with a fluffy blonde sitting in one of those easy chairs, and that very few people would believe the story, but as is I well known, dormice are good at going to sleep.

While in Calcutta, I did go to the American Crystal Unit, and frankly didn't learn a great deal except a few useful tips on the grinding process. I do remember taking an American bus to their Camp and crossing the Howrah Bridge on the way, with its forest of steel girders, but aside from that my only memory of that Camp was its toilet block. The lavatory seats were set down one side of a long hut, on a concrete dais about a foot high which ran almost the length of the building. There were ten or twelve of them, and one had the amazing spectacle of ten or a dozen Americans sitting there and trying with various degrees of physical effort and various degrees of success, to perform nature's functions, minus any form of privacy. Not a pleasant sight! On the way out was a poster showing a soldier talking to a prostitute, with a couple of little demons behind her, labelled 'Syph' and 'Gonn' saying to each other lets both gang up on this one". This reminded me of a poem which I had picked up in conversation in the mess:-

> The people of Tiflis
>
> Suffer mostly from measles
>
> While in Eritrea
>
> The trouble is usually rheumatism.

The streets of Calcutta had good old-fashioned tram cars, plus motor traffic mixed with hundreds of rickshaws and horse-drawn carts. But there were also the cows! Quite a lot of placid creamy-white animals with drooping ears were allowed to go where they pleased as the cow was a sacred animal. It often happened that a cow would just lie down on the tram lines, and then a long queue of trams would pile up, and passengers could either get out and walk or sit and wait for the cow to move, depending on how hot it was and how urgent their journey. Being near the coast it could be uncomfortably humid in that city.

RICKSHAW, LATER CONVERTED TO CYCLE-POWER, THANK GOODNESS

When I collected that big coil of cab-tyre flex (The whole object of the exercise) it was too heavy to carry far, so I took the only transport available which was a rickshaw. I sat in state, with the heavy wire under my feet, while the

Rickshaw-Wallah jogged along between the shafts in front of me ringing a small brass bell tied to one end of the shafts, to clear a way through the solid mass of urbanity ahead. It was very hot, and sweat ran down the back of that poor chap in rivulets. There and then I decided that I would never again ride in a Rickshaw if I could help it, as I felt ashamed to put a fellow man to such indignity. So next time, I took a taxi.

Calcutta taxis were something quite different. So my journey back to Dum dum Airport was in an open-topped 'Tourer' with a crew of two fearsome brigands in the front, and me in the back, plus my suitcase and about eighty pounds of thick black wire. I had been lucky enough to get a seat on an Indian Airway flight to Delhi, and was very surprised to be put on board a de Havilland Rapide, the same type as the one which had done tight turns over Cranwell some time earlier. Five of us got into the spartan interior of the Rapide, and awaited the arrival of the driver. We were not greatly encouraged when a mechanic opened each engine casing in turn, gave a cursory glance inside to see if the engine was still there, and fastened the casing up again. This we assumed to be their equivalent of the DI or Daily Inspection, which in the RAF is a well ordered and thorough check, so now we placed our hope on the legendary reliability of the machine.

The pilot arrived, the engines started first try, and without bothering even to warm up the motors we took off into the blue.

RAF 'DOMINIE' — DE HAVILAND 'RAPIDE'
AS NEAR AS I CAN REMEMBER IT

The blue turned out to be rather bumpy, and the Rapide behaves rather like a trawler in a rough sea when the air is turbulent, so most of the passengers were either white or bright green. After about an hour, the pilot turned round and seeing that I was the only one with normal colouring, he asked me to go down to the back seat and bring him a map of India which he had left there. This I did and watched with interest as he flew with one hand and manipulated the map with the other. He tried it upside down and sideways, folded in quarters and opened flat, finally dropping it on the floor and we droned on through the heat with featureless sandy landscape stretching in every direction. Then he spied an airfield ahead, and we soon found ourselves circling over a runway with dozens of Horsa gliders lined up neatly down one side. We landed and were refuelled by a team of RAF ground crew, so I got out and had a word with the Flight Sergeant in charge of operations.

"Am I allowed to ask you where we are?" I asked. "I'd rather you didn't Sir" he said with a grin, "But I've put the pilot on the right track and he should be OK soon". So once again we took off and struck South, judging by the sun, till we found a railway line which we followed for hundreds of miles, until Delhi came into view as daylight was beginning to fall. Goodness only knows where we had been, but those Horsa gliders had obviously been awaiting troop transport operations for the long-awaited push towards Japan, and we were not supposed to have seen them.

Back among the amateur theatricals, we next obtained six drain-pipes, and filled one end of each with concrete. We stood them on end on wooden planks, and filled them with salt water, and these were the dimmers for our stage lighting. As we lowered a big steel rod into each dimmer, one of the lighting circuits glowed more and more brightly, Red, Amber, Blue and White. The whole thing was terribly dangerous, and one of the pipes leaked a bit, so that some of the girls in bare feet complained that they were getting shocks. The show was a great success, but looking back its a wonder we didn't electrocute the entire cast and ourselves as well.

Even the nails required to make the scenery were a problem. Two of us made a journey into a forbidden part of the City of Old Delhi, to buy nails and screws. We hired a Tonga, or horse drawn trap, and were driven down streets so narrow that the wheels touched both sides at once. But we did get nails and screws of the right size, having gone through the famous Street of the Silversmiths, where my friend had a gold watchcase repaired to the very highest standard of craftsmanship.

DELHI "TONGA"

The Army had a Crystal Unit at Agra. and when we found that out it suddenly became very important that each member of my team should visit the Army Unit to exchange information and increase our inter-Forces co-operation, as we were often asked to provide crystals suitable for Army Transmitters and Receivers. It so happens that the Taj Mahal is located at Agra, so we all managed to see that magnificent building. By a strange coincidence, each of us managed to arrive at full-moon and saw it both by moonlight and during the day. Either way it is breath-taking in its beauty, a huge mosaic of semi-precious stones of all colours, built at the command of the Shah Jehan as a

Mausoleum and is something we will remember as long as we shall live.

THE TAJ MAHAL
AT AGRA

Only once while I was in India did I have seven days holiday. Some of my friends at the Mess had organised a week at Simla, and persuaded me to take time off and come with them. At the very last minute I got permission and managed to book accommodation. I had no reservation on the overnight train, but a few rupees paid to the train conductor got me aboard, and we trundled our way towards the foothills of the Himalayas. The final leg of the journey should have been by narrow-gauge railway which climbs about six or seven thousand feet to Simla, but again I had no reservation and the little train was chock full. So I had to make the journey in a taxi shared with five Indians who were in the same predicament, and a pretty hair-raising trip it turned out to be, with hills up and down, hairpins and wiggles all taken at high speed and hoping that nothing was coming in the opposite direction. At long last we got to Simla where I was to stay at a rather ram-shackle Officers Rest House, in a dormitory with three others, while my friends were at the Viceroy's Summer Palace in great luxury.

All the same, I would not have missed the mountain scenery for all the tea in China (which was not very far away). One day we hired bicycles and cycled miles along a rough road which was indicated by a faded signpost which read "Tibet 90 miles". We saw enormous mountains piled up as far as the eye could see, and one or two stone-built villages. One man was actually going to Tibet by the look of him. He was riding on a donkey and carrying a small parcel in front of him with great care, while about a hundred yards behind was his wife, walking along in the black cloak of Purdah which covered her from the top of her head to the ground. She was carrying a huge bundle on her head, and the picture flashed through my mind of Joseph walking while

Mary carried her precious load on the donkey for over a hundred miles to Bethlehem.

MAN AND WIFE ON THE ROAD TO TIBET

The first evening I was up there at six thousand feet, I walked up a steep path to a marvellous viewpoint, and found that the short climb had made me quite giddy after spending so long down on the plains of Indan, but soon I acclimatised and could enjoy that bracing morning air. Each morning we all met for coffee on the terraced main street. Simla is built along the face of a very steep slope, so that the buildings on one side of the road had to be supported on one side by timbers running down to the road some way below. It all looked insecure and rickety, so one morning when we were having our coffee, and when a sudden rumbling thundering noise shook the building, I was out on the street like a streak of lightning. Everybody was laughing like mad when I got back, and especially when I could tell them that I had seen four big baboon-like monkeys galloping across the corrugated iron roofs of the building, which made the noise that I immediately thought was the whole building starting to slide down the hillside. Dormice have lightning reactions and act quickly to take cover!

"MONKEY CAFE" SIMLA

When it was time to return to Delhi, I was able to organise a reservation on the narrow-gauge mountain railway, which we knew as the 'Torah peachy, Oopah neachy Railway' being roughly translated from the Hindi as 'little bit later, Up-down Railway'. Waiting with my luggage on Simla Station I could hear the train approaching long before it arrived. Although I couldn't see it, I felt sure that it was doing a good sixty miles and hour, and expected it to dash straight through the station and half way to China before it could possibly stop. When eventually it did appear, it seemed to be climbing almost vertically upwards towards us, giving out clouds of steam and making a tremendous noise, travelling at a fast walking pace. But the train ride was worth coming all that way to experience, as the train threaded its way down the hillsides with view after view of high mountains and deep valleys every bit of the way. People walking along the trackside would wave to us and we would wave back. Differences of nationality and colour were non-existent as we did what comes naturally to all sorts of people from children to pensioners, the world over.

Back in Delhi it was stifling hot on the plains, and the humidity was rising making it even more uncomfortable, and harder to do our work. But we knew that the Monsoon was on its way, and then the temperature would fall. When it reaches 100°F you are sweating from every pore, all the time, and if you should stop sweating you need medical attention before heat-stroke sets in. If it gets up to 110°F, the eyes begin to smart, and even the mynah birds sit still on fences with their mouths wide open, panting like dogs. Brain-fever birds give their maddening rising series of calls, and work becomes desperately difficult.

Then clouds began to form and towards sunset the cloudscapes were magnificent, rising to an unbelievable height in piles of cauliflower-topped cumulus, tinted with ever warmer colours as the sun went lower in the sky. I have never seen clouds of such beauty, and the air seemed crystal clear, which made my cycle ride back to the Mess in the evening an unforgettable event for a few days. But then one day as I rode back from work, there was an ominous dark line down on the windward horizon, and as I pedalled smartly the dark yellow cloud was overtaking me, reaching well overhead by the time I got to my room. It went dark, it thundered, and it went on thundering and thundering until the thunder became one continuous crashing roar. It lightened, and even the lightning became one continuous flicker of blinding light. Then it started to rain. How it rained! I took off my clothes and put on my swimming trunks and went out into that rain much to the delight of my bearer who thought I had finally gone bats.

Next morning the cycle ride was rather different. There was a basket hanging from the front of the handlebars, and this now held shoes and socks. A large yellow cycle cape covered me and the basket, so the contents kept reasonably dry, while I pedalled in bare feet and each foot went under water when the pedal was near the ground, as floods were everywhere. Nothing was dry for some weeks, and we just had to stay a trifle moist until conditions improved.

CYCLING TO WORK IN MONSOON

All around the crystal laboratory was sand, with a few thorny bushes. Only a couple of weeks or so after the rain started, we noticed one morning that a green haze was covering the acres of sandy ground, and this new green grass grew at a rate which could not be believed. Perhaps it was nine weeks later that we measured the bamboo-like grasses eight feet high behind our hut. Now that is speedy growth, and we figured that if we could develop a food crop which could grow like that, then the food shortage which seemed to be endemic could be considerably reduced, or even removed. With hindsight we can see that others did more than dream about it, and now the rice crop can come within sight of meeting the demand, but at that time many were starving.

Came a time when we heard rumours of a push toward Japan, and with the rumours came demands for more and more crystals. One huge order was for crystals to fit Naval and Army equipment so that each service unit could co-operate with the other in combined operations which we reckoned would mean a landing eventually in Japan. This we rather dreaded as it would be more difficult than the D day landings or Italy, and involve the loss of many lives, so we were rather subdued as we worked late into the night to complete the order on time. Again we sweated until drops fell from our eyebrows and nose ends, and most of our khaki drill was black, but at last the job was done on time and we thought we hadn't done too badly. The crystals were packed up and handed over to the pilot of and RAF plane flown into Willingdon Airport specially bound for Djakarta in Java. We all went straight to our charpoys to catch up on some sleep. Only a few days later, they dropped the Hiroshima bomb. This was on the 6th August 1945, and shortly afterwards another was dropped on Nagasaki, and in eight days we heard that Japan had surrendered. The war was over, but our feelings were very mixed. Our casualties had been few, but at what a cost in human death and suffering. The way our lads had been treated by the Japs made us terribly bitter but even then we were shocked at the holocaust and concerned as to the long-term results, so no one threw his hat in the air, but only heaved a sigh of relief as hostilities suddenly ended. Quite unexpectedly we found ourselves at peace after six years of war.

CHAPTER 9

Many thousands of men now had to be returned to the UK and discharged from the armed forces. Vast organisations had to be set up to cope with this new problem. How do you produce a hundred thousand men's suits, for instance, to kit men out for civilian life again? It was many months later that we received orders from Air Ministry to pack up the equipment and despatch it to the UK, and then to return ourselves. At the time, we were glad to see the back of it all and our consuming wish was to go home to our families and forget the war. But looking back I missed the companionship of six amazingly clever and determined friends, and wished that we could have continued the work in England rather than pack all the gear up and say 'Goodbye' to it and to each other, never to meet again.

My own exit from Delhi was quite exciting. By that time, the words 'QUIT INDIA' were painted on walls everywhere. and it was quite evident that our presence was not required and that the British Raj had 'Had it'. So when the big day came, and six junior officers were sitting on top of their luggage on the back of a lorry, they had fun getting from New Delhi to the station which is in Old Delhi. Near the Red Fort there were trees at regular intervals beside the road, each surrounded by an open lattice of bricks to keep the cows off. The local 'Quit India' enthusiasts had only to pick up these bricks and knock them in half to provide a useful arsenal of ammunition which was hurled at us as we passed. We did escape injury, by good fortune and some bad aiming, and with big sighs of relief we boarded the train after seeing our trunks and hand luggage into the van. Before the train started a big explosion shook the whole station, and I later learned that there was a bomb under a nearby train, which was a farewell gesture on the part of the activists, probably intended for us.

SPEEDING THE PARTING BRITISH WITH A FEW SPARE BRICKS!

The train took us back to Bombay, and to Worli Camp again, where we waited for some weeks before our turn came to embark. This time it was not new and exciting, and I only went into Bombay once or twice to buy some carved ivory elephants to take home. Once only I visited a local club which offered us hospitality. and which had a lovely swimming pool. The pool I did enjoy, though the path round it was so hot that it literally burned my bare feet. But the club members were not my type at all, and it did not help good relations when I only drank Nimbu pani instead of the hard stuff, so one visit was enough. Pukha Sahibs with their exaggerated Oxford accents were not my favourite. No wonder the Indians wanted us to quit.

For the last time in India, we packed up our suit cases and folded up our mosquito nets, when orders came to embark for home. Down the miles of seafront promenade with beautiful Western style buildings all the way along, and down to the docks again for a last look at the India Gate before going aboard the Berengaria (I think that's the right name) for a three weeks trip to normality. By now we had all got a deep sun tan and nothing on the journey was a novelty. Behind us were the twin ulcers of Hiroshima and Nagasaki, and we still wondered whether atom bombs would solve anything in the long run although we knew not a thing about carcinoma and fall-out. We just hoped for a world of freedom and progress, not realising the problems still facing us like the Berlin wall and the Japanese aftermath.

On our way through the Mediterranean we played hundreds of games of patience, and the general complaint was that they so rarely 'Came out', so I invented a new game, which came out every time, so long as you kept to the rules. It was a two-day wonder, after which no one played patience much, because they were too busy being seasick, as we had hit bad weather in the Med. and everything was going either up or down. It was colder too and we were all back into blue uniforms long before we passed Gibraltar and headed north in the far from flat Atlantic Ocean. Occasionally we caught sight of the coast of Spain, or saw the lights during the night, until one day we found ourselves slowly edging our way up the Mersey, and tied up near the Royal Liver Building at Liverpool.

But we could not go ashore because we had a case of some infectious disease on board, rumoured to be Scarlet Fever. So we just leaned over the rail and stared at Liverpool and waited, and waited and waited. For the thousands of Other Ranks on the lower decks, sleeping in hammocks with no privacy and (I thought) insufficient ventilation, it was infuriating to have to stay within sight of the island that we thought we might never see again, and not be allowed to land.

Then some customs officers came aboard and we declared any dutiable items in our kit (Or failed to do so in some predictable instances) and some time later we staggered down the gangway each carrying our hand luggage, and got into a genuine British train for the first time for years. While waiting to disembark, we had listened to a lecture about infectious diseases, and if any of us became ill we were told to consult a doctor at once. Now if anyone tells me that the dreaded Grinklewart Fever starts with a bad cough and a headache, you can bet your boots that I will wake up the very next day with a bad cough and a headache. True to form, I did not feel too well as I was processed through the system which changed me back from a Flying Dormouse to a shopkeeper. Clad in a discharge suit and looking exactly the same as thousands of other discharge suits, carrying my outsize suit case, I used up my very last First Class travel voucher and headed for Scarborough. Not that I got there straight away. By then it was obvious that I was running a temperature, shivers, headache and everything, so I left the train at York, trudged across to the Station Hotel and went straight to bed after phoning home and telling them that I would turn up when it seemed safe to do so. I did not want to take home anything like an infectious tropical disease, as my daughter was around five or six years old. That night for the only time in my life I heard a gentle knock on my bedroom door. Probably the National Association of Hotel Tarts paying me a visit, I thought, and I yelled "Go away I've got Yellow Fever", which made my headache worse but had the desired effect of stopping the door-knocker from persisting. Not that she had the slightest chance of doing any business because I never had sex with anyone except my wife, and having maintained that standard through a war I was not going to spoil it now. Also I was a Christian, very much in love with my wife, and I remained so (Boring though it may seem to succeeding generations) till the day she died, and afterwards.

Next morning things looked quite different. The temperature had gone, the world looked brighter, breakfast in the most impressive dining room of the Station Hotel tasted remarkably good, and I phoned home, paid my bill and used the very last portion of that final First Class ticket, being met at Scarborough by Marjorie and Elizabeth. From that time on I seemed to forget all about infectious diseases. Your Flying Dormouse always was a shocking worrier and a sort of cheerful pessimist. Thus closed the career of Flying

Officer Taylor F.D. 1485849, and now prithee hearken to the history of Frank Taylor, returned shopkeeper.

POST WW2 NEW SHOP-FRONT

Shopkeeping in the post-war period was not all that easy, but there was considerable satisfaction in developing our assets and increasing our turnover. We moved our small wholesale department away to other premises, and completely rebuilt the ground floor and basement, fitting it out in light oak display units and putting in a new shop front with seven window displays.

The things we sold included stationery for home and office, artists' materials, school and students' stationery, greeting cards, a small selection of books, and lots of pottery and gift lines. We still lived 'Over the shop' for some time until we had paid for the refitting, but then we were within sight of building a house in a very attractive area outside the town.

Now we had one girl at school and another little one coming along. The middle of town was no place for them to play about in, even then, so we were very glad to be able to move away, even though the road was not built up and was a row of potholes in mud. Three days after moving in , when we scarcely knew where anything was, the youngsters both went down with measles and we both had a hectic time and kept our family doctor busy too. Dr. Flatley was a charming lady who turned up with a gorgeous kitten for us, half Persian, ginger, and the other half mostly claws. The kitten I mean, not the doctor. Known as 'Rusty' it developed into a huge animal, proud and haughty, who would only eat one brand of cat food and needed lots of it. Rusty would sit at the window and watch for birds, and when he saw one close at hand (Or at paw) through the glass, his lower jaw would chatter noiselessly and he would pop round to the back door to be let out to do some serious 'Catting'. He was well disposed to children, but only tolerated adults as a necessary inconvenience, and if either of our young folk was ill he would jump onto the bed beside them and stay there all day purring like a car engine.

Came the Coronation of Queen Elizabeth II, and we did not own a television, although they were being made and sold in their thousands. However, our next door neighbours did have one, and they invited us all in to see the ceremony (In black-and-white of course) as it actually happened 240 miles away in London. Little did we then guess what influence that square box would have on the life-style and thought processes of our generation. TV aerials at that time were in the form of a five foot high letter H, mounted above the roof of the house by being clamped to the chimney stack. Every time a good gale blew up there would be dozens of chimney stacks wrecked and aerials blown down, but when colour TV came along aerials were a different shape, and a bit less perilous to chimney stacks. Then more recently the local TV repeater stations in most towns have meant that many aerials can be mounted in lofts out of sight. So TV aerials came - and went!

Our shop had a staff of ten to twelve, and made steady but unspectacular profits. We could afford to run a car, but it had to be a Morris Minor shooting brake which could be used each day to deliver goods to customers. Then we bought a Jowett van, which was still being made with a two-cylinder engine, and we had a family car as well. The busy season in the shop was from June to September, so our holidays, and those of the staff, had to be taken before or after this period. One year two friends of ours, Denis and Madge Middleton, took Marjorie and me to Switzerland in their large Austin 16 car, and we were well and truly bitten by the bug of continental travel. Since that time we have been either with friends, with children, or by ourselves, to France, Switzerland, Italy, Austria, Holland and Norway, not to mention Guernsey, Shetlands and the Isles of Scilly.

That first Swiss holiday had to be done on a tight budget. We could only take out of the country £25 plus a petrol allowance per person, and that had to last us well over a week for hotel bills and everything except the cost of the ferry crossing which was pre-paid. There were no drive-on ferries, so each car had to be slung aboard separately by a dockside crane, which was fun to watch but took an age to complete. Heavy vehicles simply did not cross the channel. Money was so tight that we loaded up the car with petrol before we put it on the boat, and each night we had a solemn committee meeting to see what we could afford to do the next day. It seems unbelievable now, but we could usually go to a small hotel and get dinner bed and breakfast for less then £2.50 each, and often a lot less. We certainly could not afford to go to the top of the Jungfrau, but we did manage a trip up the magnificent Firstbahn chairlift, and all the hotel-keepers knew that the impoverished Englishers wanted the cheapest rooms. It took all our ingenuity, plus a few five pound notes secreted here and there by mistake, to land us back in England with enough money to buy petrol for the drive home, with a bite of food on the way.

BEFORE ROLL-ON FERRIES ARRIVED, EACH CAR WAS LIFTED ABOARD BY CRANE.

I never did get up to the summit of the Jungfrau, because later on when I could afford the rail fare I was unfit to risk the journey due to heart trouble. But Interlaken is still my favourite place for magnificent scenery, and I look back with great pleasure to some wonderful holidays in the Bernese Oberland.

When we had a holiday in Norway, our son must have been around twelve years old, and we were due to move from one hotel to another, which involved a long boat journey along the fine Norwegian Fiords. Perhaps he was a little carried away by the tremendous variety of food at the breakfast table in the Hotel, but by mid-day he had turned green, had powerful stomach pains, and was very bilious. We were on the boat with the rest of the party on a package-deal holiday, and things did look rather bad. After yet another visit with Graeme to the Gent's Loo, I left him with Marjorie, I went on deck to get a little fresh air and to say a short but heart-felt prayer for help, as I knew that when we landed, we had an hour's bus ride to the journey's end. I wondered whether we should leave the party and seek medical help, or battle on with the bus trip.

Still undecided, I went round the deck and saw another member of our party sitting with his wife, and asked him what he would do in my place. It turned out that he was a doctor and he had some medicines with him, and he kept Graeme from further sickness until we reached our destination. Some would say that it was coincidence, but to me it was as plain an answer to prayer as I have known, and believe me, I was mighty thankful.

The Norwegian Doctor had Graeme back on his feet after a day in bed, and the Hotel proprietor was most helpful. The latter was called Mr. Bugge Neiss, and you can guess how that was pronounced. There was another instance of S.O.S. prayer being answered, but this time it wasn't me who was in trouble. Marjorie and I had helped Rev. Malcolm Willey to set up the Samaritans service in Scarborough, both by decorating the Samaritan's Scarborough office, and by training and serving on the team. At the time, there were not many who could man the office during working hours, and one day Marjorie was doing a spell in the office by herself, and I was at home. Suddenly I was aware that she might just be in danger, and immediately I grabbed the phone and asked her if she would like me to come to the office right then and there. The reply was "Yes please" in a steady but tense voice, so in less than ten minutes I was letting myself into the office and looking into the interview room. There I saw a man who was just removing from his wallet one of those stiff-backed razor-blades, with a pretty nasty look on his face. When he saw that Marjorie was not alone, he looked at me, looked at Marjorie, looked at the razor-blade, and putt it back into the wallet, so I suggested a cup of coffee all round might be a good idea, and the tension was broken. No wonder Marjorie's voice had been tense, and we both sweat a lot until we had got him to talk out his troubles, drink some more coffee, and seen him leave the office in a quieter frame of mind, knowing that someone actually cared.

Telepathy may be a very controversial subject, but at the time I was sure that a cry for help came quite clearly to me from my wife who desperately needed someone's intervention. Or it might have had an element of 'Answer to prayer' in it, because you pray pretty desperately if somebody is threatening you with a razor-blade.

Eventually, when the Team had got onto its feet, we both found that the Samaritan's clients were taking so much out of us that our health was suffering, and we were both advised to leave it to folk who were younger, or had thicker skins. But if you want a life-saving job, see if the Samaritans will let you join them. It's not that easy to get in.

The day to day work in the shop was getting more and more arduous. Many days it was necessary to go back to do office work after evening meal. Much of this consisted of ordering items specially to customer's requirements, as each day we would receive many such demands over the counter. Slowly I came to the conclusion that these 'Special Orders' were ruining my home life although we thought them necessary to prevent customers from going to other shops. I was working out a scheme for cutting these out completely, and making some departments 'Self-service' to reduce staff, when I got a deep-vein thrombosis and had to go to bed for several weeks.

Marjorie was just terrific. She made breakfast, went to the shop (Being given a lift by a neighbour) came home and made lunch, went back to run the business and did the washing and cleaning at night. A tough job for her in spite of wonderful help from the shop staff, and I was frustrated by enforced idleness. We got the central-heating boiler converted from coke to gas, and had a gas fire in the lounge, to avoid carrying coal and coke, but when I remember that all the meals had to be carried up fourteen stairs, I wonder how on earth she did it.

IN BED WITH TICKER PROBLEMS.

Then I was allowed to get up and eventually to go downstairs, and even walk in the garden. Each day I walked a bit further, until one day I came back feeling strangely out of breath and with slight chest pains. The Doctor called in a specialist whose diagnosis was cardiac thrombosis, and he put me back to bed for another six weeks. This was one of the low points in my life and I sure was miserable.

One of my friends at work (Jack Thompson) owned two TV sets, having won a portable set in a competition. Bless him, he brought it round and lent it to me, and from then on I had something to look at when I wanted it. Obviously, as Marjorie was running the business most of the day, I was completely alone in the house as a rule and that television set was a Godsend. There were times when I wondered what would happen if I had a repeat heart attack, but the answer was fairly clear, so I thought about something else instead, and gradually I managed to inch my way back to normality.

When the time did arrive for going back to work, the writing was on the wall and I tried to sell the business as a going concern, but without success. Then one day Marjorie told me about a chat she had had with a friend of hers, whose husband had just sold his shop to Marks and Spencer, and got a good price because he happened to be next door to the M & S store. As the shop was next door to the Pavilion Hotel run by the Laughton family for years, and now owned by the millionaire property owner of Broadlands Properties. Next day I went to see him, and after many months a sale was arranged at a price that my accountant said was very good at that time. The deal included a twelve month period in which the shop stock could be turned into cash and run down to almost zero, and Marjorie and I ended up with just the two of us selling off odds and ends at give-away price and then the fittings and furniture. One day we were able to shut the door and the firm of H.O.Taylor Ltd. was wound up.

Then we went for a week's holiday in Amsterdam. We chose that city because it was flat and therefore suitable for heart cases, and we had a great holiday there, staying at the Hotel Polen on the Damrack, the main street of the city centre, which was later to be seen burning furiously on TV news programmes. It wasn't us smoking that started that fire, as we had both stopped smoking before I was ill. We sailed back from Amsterdam to Immingham on North Sea Ferries and the very next morning we learned that the Pavilion Hotel itself was going to close because of dry-rot and other serious problems with the building. So we had just got out in time.

By this time, those two folk we knew as 'The children' had grown up and left us to start lives of their own, so we had loads of time to enjoy our home life. Or so we thought. Time to complete my education, it seemed, so I took a course in the Open University and was well into the middle of it when my mother died at the age of 97, and then disaster struck when Marjorie was overtaken by cancer and died in September of 1979 after much pain. That summer was bad for me as she lay in bed. When I could get out into the garden I tried to keep it tidy, kneeling on the grass and weeding with a trowel, and often with tears streaming down my cheeks and soaking into the dry summer soil, silently.

When she was taken into hospital for tests, the presence of cancer was first diagnosed, even though we had previously asked for a second opinion and gone privately to see Mr. Bradley, the local orthopaedic surgeon who had a series of X Rays taken and pronounced the trouble as a trapped nerve. From hospital, I had her moved to Belvedere Nursing Home for greater comfort, and there followed an operation which was expected to relieve the pain, but failed to do so. There followed three weeks which I will not attempt to describe, before my dear wife, and my best pal died while I held her hand and prayed.

That was life's lowest ebb, and all I could do was to look after myself and try to look as normal as possible. A faith in Christ is literally a life-saver at such times and my good friend, and Minister of my Church, Rev. Brian Fitzpatrick, was there in the nursing home with us when Marjorie died. You can't have a better friend than that!

As time went by, I cried less frequently and could pray more coherently, but even now there are times when some memory is revived by a sight or a sound from the past, and my ageing eyes fill again.

Before the shop was closed, Major Cyril Wilson enlisted me into Hospital Broadcasting and when he died it fell to me to become Chairman of Scarborough Hospital Broadcasting Service, which also helped me over difficult years. With Hospital Radio and with my resumed Open University course I kept myself very busy, and I learned how to wash my own clothes, and to iron them. While Marjorie was in bed I had learned to do plain cooking and developed a regular weekly menu which included plenty of fresh vegetables and fruit. What with the house to keep clean and the garden always needing attention, there was not all that amount of spare time.

HOSPITAL RADIO, SCARBOROUGH
AN ABSORBING HOBBY FOR MANY YEARS

As always, my Sundays were occupied with morning and evening services, often with extra duties there connected with the various offices which I held from time to time.

Later, the church also brought me together with a like minded lass, Joan, who eventually agreed to marry me, and helped put a purpose back in life.

Yes, I did manage to get a BA degree, and both Graeme and Elizabeth came all the way up from London to the Degree Day at York University which made a wonderful day for me. But I think I was even more proud and delighted when my son got his Doctorate at London University and both Joan and I were invited to his degree day at the Albert Hall. Now that really was a day to remember, and his PhD hood and gown were a vastly impressive claret and gold creation with a floppy hat to match, which rivalled the Lord Mayor himself in grandeur. Joan and I were on the centre aisle/right at the front of the crowds of spectators, and I was able to get a photograph of Graeme receiving his award from H.R.H. Princess Anne, Chancellor of London University.

CHAPTER 10

Hindsight

A young Methodist Minister recently asked me a question. "What are your conclusions after three quarters of a century of life?". I said that I thought that civilisation had failed!.

We can put a man on the Moon, send probes to the planets, see molecules, transplant heart and lungs, fly at twice the speed of sound, and build atomic power stations and bombs. All technical achievements, all truly mind-boggling. The quality of life in the advanced countries becomes better and better and almost everyone now has a washing machine, a TV, fridge, radio, telephone, central heating, ample food and a doctor. The majority have cars as well. Millionaires are everywhere, and millions of us fly abroad for our holidays every year.

But, and it's a big but, during my lifetime civilisation has reached a point where one nation tried to exterminate another in gas-chambers, and poison gas is still used in warfare. Not far away from our huge stocks of food (As the plane flies) humans are dying all day long from starvation, and so-called civilisation is unable to bring food and water to them. Alcohol and drug abuse abounds and sex-related diseases are increasing, especially in cities.

We have also achieved massive pollution. Pollution of the air by carbon dioxide and C.F.Cs bring the civilising effect of Acid Rain and the Greenhouse Effect, which looks likely to wreck havoc with the weather and with vegetation. Pollution of the sea, by overspill of nitrate fertilisers plus untreated human sewage, industrial poisons and atomic plant effluent, all of which leaves long-term problems. Pollution of the ground by burying long-life atomic waste with a half-life of twenty four thousand years, and by systematically felling forests every single day. Those forests turn carbon dioxide into the oxygen which we need to live. Also we are quickly using up our fossil fuels.

Human beings breed worse than rabbits. Well you must admit that there are more humans than rabbits, and it seems that the attraction of sex is irresistible, so we have had a population explosion world-wide. Those unfortunate folk, the 'Inadequate' present a special problem in this respect. People who are more cautious are now limiting their families, which may result in a greater percentage of inadequacy. Terrorism is getting completely beyond control, and goes hand in hand with religious extremism.

We hear of "Caths" and "Prots" in Ireland and "Christians" and 'Muslims" in Lebanon. All religious leaders should together outlaw terrorism, and make it quite clear that killing people in order to make a political point is not any part of their faith. Take a look at the life of Mahatma Ghandi, whom I saw and admired in Delhi. He got it right.

Now consider the effect of Civilisation upon the Arts in recent years. Skip this bit if you want to, but I think it is interesting.

First a hard look at music. From Bach to Elgar, there was "Tonal" music with tune and rhythm, and the use of an eight note octave with avoidance of discord and dissonance. Further progress led to the abandonment of tune and regular rhythms, and to the use of a thirteen-note scale with close-packed chords as dissonant as possible. There is even a piano composition called 'Three minutes twenty seconds' in which there are no notes at all. Music has disintegrated, though it must be said that there are signs of a return to sanity, of late.

Artists and Sculptors have gone non-representational via 'Isms' such as Cubism and Fauve-ism, to produce vast canvasses covered by coloured geometry and the marks of bicycle tyres. Oh yes, and a pile of bricks which cost an Art Gallery many thousands of pounds.

Architecture has lost its way a bit, too. As I write, the media are quoting H.R.H Prince Charles in criticism of contemporary architecture which is quite out of touch with the social communities which the buildings should serve. In other words the buildings are un-civilised. My cousin, Jeremy Dixon, is among those architects whose work was praised by the Prince, and again there is ground for hope for the future.

Literature has proliferated to extremes. Thousands of books are published every year, with the biggest sellers being those with the most exciting sex or violence, and those which take the lid off the biggest can of worms. OK, so there are also lots of academic books, where one may enter an

Aladdin's Cave of new knowledge, but a Dickens or a Bronte --- we have not.

Sports have developed from competitions of friendly rivalries which could sublimate territorial disputes, into multi-million pound spectator extravaganzas. There is something sinister in the psychology of those chanting football crowds, which reminds me of the "Sieg-heil sieg-heils" of the Nazi crowds.

Television is the most potent influence upon the minds of the vast majority of civilised people. TV is run by the entertainment industry and journalists, who seem to have succeeded in warping the minds of millions by representing the extremes of human experience as the norm; in hate, love, sex and suffering.

The quality of human beings resulting from this process of civilisation is scarcely improving. There is one Mother Theresa in Calcutta, but hundreds of extortionists and killers in Belfast and New York. On one hand the Australian brewer can talk in billions of pounds, on the other hand the African with no food, no water, dying. On one hand the sophisticated Home Counties executive, on the other hand hundreds of uneducable thugs, victims of both heredity and environment.

Schoolteachers today must not use the word "Blackboard" or they risk facing belligerent parents bringing complaints of racialism. So it is a "Board" and not a "Blackboard". Sex is a permitted topic of conversation of education, sexual deviation is even advocated by some; brutality has long been with us from the school playground to the fox-hunt, but morals if mentioned will lose you a lot of friends.

All eyes are firmly closed to road accidents. Fifteen people will be dead tonight who were alive this morning in our country, two hundred will be seriously injured (That's a lot of people whose lives may never be the same again) and an unbelievable six hundred and sixty people will be slightly hurt, to judge from official figures for 1987. Does that make the headlines? Does it thump, and why? Because it exposes human fallibility, both in lack of car maintenance and lack of efficiency behind the wheel.

In the RAF barrack room, way back in 1940, I learned to live with chaps whose every other word was just plain filthy. Almost all of those words have since crept into the scripts of American films which lead the way in the entertainment industry. So now you can, in certain places, use words as nasty as you like.

Except one word which is never heard except in Church, and even then it is covered by a thick layer of Victorian dust. Significantly that word is "Sin".

So "Civilised" man is sophisticated, technically clever, but not wise, and certainly not very civil to his fellow human beings. Not really CIVIL-ised after developing from the apes to homo sapiens, and from tribal communities through national status and empires to super powers who have thousands of atomic warheads each (Which they dare not use after Chernobyl, because of the fall-out). Clever. but not very generous, and in my opinion there is a need to catch up on "Love they neighbour" and remember that the neighbour not only lives next door, but also in Africa.

Which brings us back to the source of that phrase "Love thy neighbour". Me, I am a denominational mongrel! Perhaps there was Jewish blood in my ancestry, or perhaps it was the doctor, but I was circumcised as a baby and then baptised into the Anglican faith at Holy Trinity Church, Scarborough. I can remember being a toddler in the Sunday School at the Bar Church (They pulled it down after that) and going there regularly to Sunday Service. Having tried all the churches I could find from Quakers to Catholics (Then a rude word to Protestants) I joined the Methodists and found a faith in God through Jesus.

Once I went to a conference of the Young Laymens' League (YLL) at Swanick (Sitting on the bench of a motor lorry all the way there). Later I helped to organise local conferences at wooden huts near Cober Hill, Cloughton, where hundreds of youngish people from the district got down to the nuts and bolts of religion. Later still I was accepted as a local preacher, though after very inadequate training, and worked every Sunday afternoon as a Sunday School teacher and even a pianist!

In middle age I became Communion Steward, Vestry Steward, (Many times) and Circuit Steward. When my church adopted Christian Stewardship, I was Chairman of that project and we had 400 people at the inaugural dinner at the Grand Hotel (Very tough Duck a l'orange). But the inadequacy of my training as a preacher was brought home by life in the RAF, and I declined to take services thereafter.

I am completely convinced that Jesus did live, and that he died a tortured death in demonstration of the nature of God in human terms. It is not easy for us to think back two thousand years, into the thought-forms and customs of a Middle Eastern country under foreign occupation. There was no printing, everything was hand-written or committed to memory, and at times both then and since there were additions and embroidery, but there is a timeless quality in the four Synoptic Gospels if we read them without prejudices. There is down to earth wisdom in the stories of the Good Samaritan and the Prodigal Son. The words of the Lord's Prayer were those taught by Jesus to his disciples (Though, the final phrases may have been a later addition) and we should take a cold hard look at them. Jesus also confirmed two of the Ten Commandments as paramount, "You must love the Lord your God" and "Love your neighbour as yourself". That's enough to start with, work through that lot and wise up to the meaning of Christianity.

Theology is its own worst enemy, and has produced a language all its own which is unintelligible and off-putting, to around eighty five percent of folk on these islands. It has also in the past resulted in religious extremism, and splits in the church. Avoid religious extremists of all persuasions, as they are often used by terrorist factions to generate popular support for their activities. Denominations are now moving closer together, with certain interesting exceptions, but my advice is to hunt out a church where they worship God in the way that you want to worship God. If they later alter the service so that you can't worship properly, go somewhere else where you can! There's plenty of choice from the slap-happy gospel songs to Gregorian Chants, so forget denominational differences and go right back to the facts and parables of the New Testament. That way there is a reason for living and a slight hope that humanity can survive.

Golly! Some of us Dormice do go on a bit, don't we!

Printed in the United Kingdom
by Lightning Source UK Ltd.
108685UKS00001B/289-306